PAT BROWN, MBA

Unwinding Concentrated Stock

"Financial Literacy Strategies for Protecting and Growing Your Wealth"

ABRAM 47 BROWN

First published by AbramBrown47 2025

First edition

ISBN: 978-1-967737-41-3

This book was professionally typeset on Reedsy.
Find out more at reedsy.com

Contents

Preface

If you're reading this, chances are you hold something rare — and something powerful.

A concentrated stock position.

Maybe it's from the company you helped build from the ground up. Maybe it's from a long, distinguished career as a public company executive. Maybe it's the reward for being an early employee who bet on a vision before the market caught up. Maybe it's the result of diligent saving, investing heavily in a company you believed in long before it made headlines.

Whatever your path, you now find yourself with a significant portion of your net worth tied up in the stock of one company.

And with that privilege comes risk — the kind of risk most investors never have to face. The kind of risk that demands more than just generic advice. The kind of risk that demands precision, strategy, and a deep understanding of what's really at stake.

This is a book for people like you.

People who are smart, capable, and successful — but who may not have been taught how to navigate wealth at this level. People who know how to create value, drive results, and lead organizations — but who now need a different kind of leadership: leadership over their own wealth.

You're not just managing a portfolio anymore.

You're managing a future.

Why This Book?

Unwinding Concentrated Stock isn't about trading strategies. It isn't about market forecasts or stock picking.

It's about the reality of holding too much of one thing — even if that one thing made you rich.

Concentration is how wealth is created.

Diversification is how wealth is preserved.

The journey from creation to preservation is not intuitive. It's not easy. It's not obvious. And it's not always comfortable — especially when the stock in question feels like more than an investment. It feels like a story. A loyalty. A belief.

But here's the truth:

Markets don't care about your story.

Markets don't reward loyalty.

Markets move — often irrationally, and always unpredictably.

And if too much of your financial life is tied to one company's fortunes, you are exposed. Not just to price swings, but to existential risks — risks that, left unmanaged, can erase years of hard work and smart decisions in a single market cycle.

This book exists to help you prevent that.

To help you unwind, not just emotionally, but strategically.

To help you diversify without regret.

To help you protect what you've built — and amplify it for the future.

Who This Book Is For

Let's be clear: this book is not just for founders and business owners.

It's for anyone with a concentrated position in individual stock:

Public company executives whose compensation packages include significant stock grants or options.

Early employees who earned equity in companies that have since gone public or been acquired.

Corporate professionals who accumulated company stock over decades through stock purchase plans, bonuses, and loyalty.

Angel investors and venture capitalists who made early bets that paid off — in concentrated form.

Family wealth inheritors who find themselves owning large stakes in a single legacy company.

Founders and entrepreneurs, of course — but not only them.

If a single stock makes up a significant chunk of your net worth — if you live or die financially by the movements of one ticker symbol — this book is for you.

It doesn't matter how you got here.

It matters where you go next.

The Double-Edged Sword of Concentration

Owning a lot of one stock can feel safe — especially if that stock got you where you are today.

You know the company.

You trust the leadership.

You believe in the mission.

You've watched the stock climb. Maybe you've even felt smarter, more validated, more secure because of it.

But here's the problem: the very familiarity that makes you comfortable also makes you vulnerable.

Concentration risk is insidious because it doesn't feel risky — until it is.

You don't notice it day to day, quarter to quarter.

You notice it all at once.

You notice it when a regulatory change slashes market cap by 30%.

When a CEO scandal sends shockwaves through the stock price.

When a new competitor launches an innovation you didn't see coming.

When macroeconomic factors — a recession, an interest rate hike, a geopolitical event — crush valuations across the board.

Concentration magnifies all these risks.

It turns normal market volatility into personal financial earthquakes.

And yet, unwinding is hard.

Emotionally.

Strategically.

Financially.

Because there's tax to consider. There's timing. There are market optics, insider trading windows, public filings. There are psychological biases — overconfidence, anchoring, loss aversion — that make selling feel like betrayal.

This book is here to help you through all of that.

What This Book Will Teach You

Unwinding Concentrated Stock is a playbook — not a lecture.

It's designed to equip you with the frameworks, strategies, and real-world tools you need to:

Assess the true risk of your concentration — not just mathematically, but practically.

Design a customized diversification plan based on your goals, your time horizon, and your risk tolerance.

Execute tax-efficient selling strategies to minimize what you owe and maximize what you keep.

Use advanced tools — 10b5-1 plans, collars, exchange funds, prepaid forwards — to unwind without flooding the market or tripping legal wires.

Build a long-term wealth management plan that integrates investment strategy, estate planning, philanthropy, and legacy building.

Manage the emotions that come with unwinding — so you don't sabotage yourself at the most critical moment.

Communicate effectively with your advisors — wealth managers, tax strategists, estate attorneys — to ensure coordination and execution.

Avoid the traps that have caught even the smartest, wealthiest people off guard.

You'll learn from case studies, examples, and decades of experience advising people exactly like you — people who sat where you sit now, facing decisions that would shape the rest of their financial lives.

The Cost of Inaction

It's tempting to do nothing.

To tell yourself, "I'll wait for a better time."

"I'll unwind when the stock hits that next milestone."

"I'll diversify after this next earnings call."

But the cost of waiting is invisible — until it isn't.

And when it isn't, it's catastrophic.

I've seen fortunes evaporate because of inaction.

I've seen decades of work undone because of hesitation.

I've seen families inherit less, foundations launch smaller, dreams shrink — not because people didn't care, but because they didn't plan.

You didn't get where you are by leaving things to chance.

Don't leave this to chance either.

A New Mindset

If there's one thing I want you to walk away from this book with, it's a new mindset about wealth.

Wealth isn't static.

It's not a trophy to be admired or a number to be preserved.

It's dynamic.

It needs to be managed, evolved, stewarded.

It needs to work for you — not trap you.

Unwinding concentrated stock isn't about "getting out."

It's about leveling up.

It's about transforming the concentrated wealth you created into the diversified, resilient, empowered wealth that will carry you — and your family, your causes, your legacy — forward.

Final Words Before We Begin

This isn't a book about fear.

It's a book about freedom.

Freedom from market whiplash.

Freedom from concentration anxiety.

Freedom to dream bigger, invest smarter, and live more intentionally.

Freedom to turn the incredible achievement of concentrated success into the even more incredible achievement of lasting impact.

If that sounds like the future you want — you're in the right place.

Let's Get Something Clear Before We Begin

If you're holding this book, it's because you already understand something that most investors never confront: real wealth isn't just about how many shares you own, or how many zeros trail your portfolio balance. It's not about a single stock price ticking up on a Bloomberg terminal. It's not about bragging rights at the country club. Wealth — serious wealth — is about something far bigger, far more intricate.

It's about control.

It's about stewardship.

And most importantly, it's about responsibility.

You see, when you hold a concentrated stock position — whether you earned it through decades of loyalty at a public company, through an IPO at a firm you helped build, through equity compensation, or even a windfall from an early investment — you are not just another investor playing a game of numbers. You're playing on a different field entirely.

Most people define wealth with a number. Maybe it's $5 million. Maybe it's $50 million. Maybe it's a hundred million or more. But at your level, the number itself becomes irrelevant. What matters is what that concentrated wealth gives you — and what it demands of you.

It gives you options others will never have: options to start businesses without asking permission, options to fund the causes you care about, options to buy back your time and design your life with precision. But it also demands something most will never face: the need to manage risk that isn't abstract but personal. The need to unwind exposure, not because you're pessimistic, but because you're pragmatic. The need to transform an asset that once built your wealth into a diversified platform that preserves it.

Let's begin with the real asset here: control.

When you're sitting on a large, concentrated position in one company, you are not in control — the market is. The company's quarterly earnings are. Interest rates are. Regulatory shifts are. One announcement, one lawsuit, one management misstep, and the asset you've been counting on for your future can lose 20%, 30%, or 50% of its value before you can even react.

Control over your wealth comes not from holding tightly, but from moving strategically. From diversifying intelligently. From unwinding risk while preserving opportunity. Concentration created your wealth. But diversification will protect it — and extend it into the future.

Beyond control, real wealth — and particularly concentrated wealth — carries a responsibility.

You may have once thought that responsibility was just to yourself: to maximize your returns, to optimize your tax strategy. But now, it's broader. You have a responsibility to your family. To the next generation. To your future self who will one day want stability more than another roll of the dice.

We're not talking about the next quarter. Or even the next year. We're talking about the next 50 years. About the next 100. This isn't just financial planning — this is legacy engineering.

Because here's the reality: concentrated stock is volatile by nature. Companies rise — and fall. Market darlings today can be old news tomorrow. Without a plan to transition your concentrated position into something sturdier, you're gambling with a legacy that took a lifetime to build.

Now, let's talk about what wealth really buys you at this level: optionality.

Wealth buys you the ability to design your life. To walk away from things that no longer serve you. To say yes to what inspires you and no to what doesn't. Wealth, properly managed, buys you freedom. But that freedom is fragile if it's sitting atop a single asset. Options require flexibility, and flexibility requires liquidity. And liquidity only comes through careful, strategic unwinding.

If you manage it well, you buy back time. You buy back energy. You buy back the ability to focus on the things that matter most — family, legacy, impact, health, purpose. If you manage it poorly — if you cling to the stock because of fear, nostalgia, ego, or inertia — you risk losing all of it.

Eventually — and inevitably — the real question shifts.

It's not "How much is this stock worth today?"

It's "What kind of life am I building with what I have?"

It's "What will I leave behind?"

Because true wealth isn't the number you post on a balance sheet. It's the values you instill. It's the culture you create. It's the opportunities you preserve for your children and their children. It's the impact you make long after your stock has stopped trading.

Here's what very few people will tell you: with great wealth comes not just opportunity but stewardship.

Ownership says, "This is mine."

Stewardship says, "This is my responsibility."

Ownership clings. Stewardship cultivates.

Ownership chases returns. Stewardship builds resilience.

The ultra-wealthy who find true satisfaction understand this difference deeply. They know that wealth is not a static trophy but a dynamic tool. They recognize that wealth demands attention, expertise, and deliberate action. That without a plan, even the largest fortune can erode in a generation — not from extravagance or scandal, but from simple neglect.

And when you hold concentrated stock, that neglect doesn't just mean volatility — it means vulnerability.

If you think wealth is about accumulation, you stay stuck. Reactive. Exposed. Waiting for the markets to be kind. But if you understand that wealth at this level is about transformation — about turning fragile concentration into durable diversification — you free yourself to focus on what truly matters: living well and leaving well.

This is the difference between being merely wealthy and being powerful.

Not loud power. Not flashy power. Quiet, enduring power.

The power that shapes lives. That builds industries. That fortifies families for generations.

The kind of power that doesn't show up in headlines — but does show up in legacies.

The kind of power that frees your children to pursue purpose without being shackled by entitlement.

The kind that doesn't just preserve wealth — it preserves meaning.

Wealth is a platform, not a prison. Handled well, it offers freedom, peace, and purpose. Handled poorly, it can feel like golden handcuffs — shining, but binding. The difference isn't in how much you have. It's in how well you steward it.

So here's the first real question I want you to consider before we dive deeper:

Are you managing your concentrated wealth — or mastering it?

Are you sitting on it, hoping the market stays kind — or are you building something deliberate, durable, resilient?

Are you playing defense — or are you designing offense?

Because concentrated wealth without a plan is a liability.

But concentrated wealth with a plan?

It's a legacy.

And the world doesn't need more people clinging to stock certificates.

It needs more stewards. More builders. More architects of lasting impact.

You didn't work this hard to gamble with your future.

The World Sees Wealth and Assumes Simplicity

The world sees concentrated stock wealth and assumes ease. It assumes security. It assumes arrival. As if the mere presence of a substantial portfolio — heavily weighted in a single stock — means the journey is over, and the hard work is done. You and I know better.

Wealth — particularly concentrated wealth — doesn't simplify life; it complicates it. It doesn't resolve uncertainty; it amplifies it. What the outside world calls "success" often marks, for those truly living it, the beginning of a more complex chapter — one that demands more discipline, more strategic thinking, and a far deeper kind of leadership.

The moment you shift from accumulation to preservation, from risk-taking to risk management, the real work begins. These aren't the struggles the media talks about. They're quieter, heavier, and far more complex — lived under the surface of every individual sitting on a concentrated stock position.

Let's step into those real dilemmas — the ones hiding behind the headlines.

Complexity vs. Simplicity

At the early stages of wealth-building, the formula feels clean: earn more, save more, invest consistently. Your net worth rises as your single-stock holding grows. Success, seemingly, is measured by how high the stock price climbs.

But as your holdings mature and your wealth scales, simplicity gives way to complexity. Concentrated wealth breeds concentrated risk. At some point, a realization hits: you're not diversified. Your entire financial future is tied to the performance of a single company — its leadership, its market sector, its quarterly reports.

Suddenly, it's not just about *how much* you have; it's about *how vulnerable* you are.

Add in layers of planning: tax consequences, stock options, RSUs, charitable giving vehicles, estate plans, maybe even a donor-advised fund or a family office. Each layer is built for protection — but each adds complexity.

The greatest risk isn't the stock price falling. It's complexity mutating into paralysis. Structures that were meant to free you instead trap you — in tax consequences you didn't anticipate, in estate structures that don't flex, in liquidity crises at the worst possible times.

Mastery here is not about more complexity. It's about clarity.

True wealth management isn't about how many strategies you have. It's about having the *right* ones — lean, efficient, and aligned to your purpose.

Privacy vs. Isolation

Wealth brings options, and one of the first luxuries it affords is privacy. The ability to step out of the public eye, to shield your life from unwanted scrutiny.

But walls built for privacy can turn into walls of isolation.

When you've built substantial wealth — particularly when it's wrapped up in a high-profile stock — you begin to wonder: who do I trust? Who knows me for me, not for my portfolio?

Old friendships strain. New relationships feel transactional. Family dynamics can become fraught — inheritance, expectations, unspoken resentments. You start questioning motives: Are they here for me, or for what they think I can give?

The danger is real. Left unaddressed, privacy becomes loneliness. Discretion becomes disconnection.

The antidote isn't withdrawing further — it's intentional curation.

It's about building a circle — small, trusted, values-driven — where you are known not as a ticker symbol but as a person. Where wealth isn't a barrier or a magnet but simply a detail.

Because no amount of financial freedom matters if you feel trapped behind the gates you built yourself.

Opportunity vs. Risk

Wealth opens doors. So many doors.

Access to elite investment deals. Private equity opportunities. Venture capital rounds. Family office direct investments. Invitations to syndicates, partnerships, boards.

The influx is relentless. But here's the hard truth: not every opportunity is an *opportunity*.

Ultra-affluence, particularly concentrated affluence, draws opportunists like moths to a flame. Deals promising outsized returns with suspiciously little risk. Startups that are "can't-miss." Investment pitches that prey on your success story.

The skill here isn't in saying *yes* — it's in learning to say *no* — and meaning it.

It's learning that restraint is a superpower. That the best opportunities often aren't the loudest, flashiest, or most urgent. That good deals aren't made under pressure.

Mastery means evaluating opportunities with a clear lens: Is this aligned with my strategy? Is this aligned with my mission? Or is it simply chasing return for return's sake?

Wealth isn't about saying yes to everything you *can* do. It's about saying yes only to what you *should* do.

Legacy vs. Entitlement

You want your wealth to last. To matter. To serve. To free your family, not trap them.

But you've seen the headlines: second-generation wealth squandered.

Third-generation wealth forgotten. Legacies, once proud, dissolving into entitlement.

The great paradox of concentrated stock wealth is this: what built your fortune — focus, risk, patience — is not what preserves it across generations.

Preservation requires something different: education, communication, stewardship.

Your goal isn't just to pass along money. It's to pass along mindset. Values. Responsibility.

Because wealth, without wisdom, becomes a weight. A burden. A slow erosion of ambition.

True legacy is not what you leave *to* your heirs — it's what you leave *in* them.

Financial literacy. Emotional resilience. Stewardship, not entitlement.

The work begins now — not later. The conversations must start while you're alive, while you can guide them, model them, live them.

Why This Matters

Recognizing these tensions doesn't solve them.

But recognizing them is the beginning of mastery.

If you have a concentrated stock position, you're holding more than wealth — you're holding risk, complexity, responsibility, and opportunity in its most distilled form.

Those who succeed in unwinding concentrated stock — who protect their wealth and extend their legacy — aren't just savvy investors. They are intentional leaders. They are stewards.

Because the real challenge isn't managing the market's volatility.

It's managing the volatility of life itself — family, relationships, mission, meaning.

That's why I wrote *Unwinding Concentrated Stock* — not to help you make a few more percentage points on your returns, but to help you master the deeper game.

This is about converting fragile wealth into fortified legacy.

This is about trading accidental fortune for deliberate impact.

This is about leading — not just investing.

The Call to Action

If you're holding this book, you're already ahead of the game.

But awareness is not action.

Understanding without action is the first step toward regret.

So here's your simple challenge:

Identify one area — complexity, isolation, opportunity, or legacy — where you know you're exposed.

Write it down. Be honest. No one else needs to see it.

And then: commit to one small, deliberate action this week.

Maybe it's calling your financial advisor to discuss diversification.

Maybe it's scheduling a family meeting about values and legacy.

Maybe it's saying "no" to the next investment pitch that doesn't fit.

Maybe it's revisiting your estate plan.

One move. This week.

Because concentrated wealth is not self-managing. It demands stewardship. It demands leadership.

And most of all — it demands action.

How to use this book

If you've made it this far, let's set the right expectation: this isn't a novel. It's not a breezy read meant to entertain you or a feel-good manual selling overnight breakthroughs. It's not a lecture on what you "should have done" or a guilt trip about what you have now. This book is a guide — a manual — for the very real, very high-stakes challenges of managing concentrated wealth.

It's built not for speed, but for precision. It's for individuals like you — individuals with real stakes, real decisions to make, real complexity to unwind. People who don't need more noise or complexity — but sharper tools, better frameworks, and the right questions at the right time.

You don't have to read this book front to back. In fact, I would caution against it. Wealth — and especially concentrated stock wealth — isn't linear, and neither is this book. Move through it the way you move through your financial life: intentionally, strategically, with clear purpose. Each chapter is designed as a standalone field guide. Each principle is a tool, not a lecture. Each section is designed to deliver real-world action, not academic theory.

This isn't entertainment. You won't find endless graphs or confusing charts here. No jargon designed to impress — only insights meant to serve. This book is a reference, a blueprint, a survival manual for navigating the opportunities and risks of concentrated wealth. It's the guide you'll wish you had when you're staring at an expiring stock option, a looming liquidity event, a volatile market shift, or a family meeting about legacy planning.

It's a book you'll return to — not because it's long, but because it's relevant. As your life evolves, as your wealth grows, as the complexity multiplies, this book will meet you exactly where you are.

How to Navigate This Book

Start Where You Are: Begin by scanning the table of contents. Find the chapter that hits you hardest — the issue keeping you up at 3 a.m., or the decision you know is waiting around the corner. Start there. Relevance matters more than sequence.

Use It Like a Toolkit: Are you considering how to unwind a concentrated stock position? Start with the liquidity chapters. Worried about tax exposure on highly appreciated assets? Dive into the tax mitigation strategies. Thinking about transferring wealth to the next generation? Head to the family governance and legacy planning sections. This book is designed to flex to your life — not the other way around.

Come Back Often: Wealth management — especially when concentrated — isn't a one-and-done task. As your company evolves, as markets shift, as laws change, new decisions will surface. This book is built to be your compass — a resource that evolves with you.

Act As You Go: Don't treat this like an academic exercise. Apply one idea. Make one decision. Adjust one habit. Take one meeting with an advisor. Momentum matters more than perfection. In wealth — as in life — action creates clarity.

What You'll Find Inside

Clarity Over Complexity: Sophisticated wealth strategies don't have to be buried in dense, unreadable technical language. We translate complexity into clarity — not because you can't understand it, but because it's far more powerful when you can act on it.

Principles Over Prescriptions: There's no one-size-fits-all formula for managing concentrated wealth. You don't need cookie-cutter advice — you need frameworks that flex. You'll find principles here, not rigid checklists.

Action Over Theory: Each chapter ends with tangible action steps — not theory, not hypothetical best-case scenarios. Practical, real-world moves you can make right now.

Freedom Over Fear: Wealth — even concentrated wealth — shouldn't feel like a trap. It should enable freedom. Every section is built to help you regain control, reduce anxiety, and align your money with your mission.

A Note on Style

This book is intentionally clean. No endless footnotes. No jargon for the sake of sounding smart. No filler. Just clear, honest, direct conversation — the way you'd expect from a trusted advisor.

Imagine sitting across from someone who understands both the complexity of your wealth and the simplicity of your goals: dignity, autonomy, legacy. That's the voice of this book.

Direct. Respectful. Actionable.

Final Thought

This isn't about chasing more. You already have *more*. More assets. More complexity. More options.

This is about mastering what you've already earned.

It's about turning concentrated wealth into diversified strength. It's about using your financial position not just to build a portfolio, but to build a life — one defined by clarity, freedom, and legacy.

It's about ensuring that what you spent decades building doesn't become a liability, but a platform — for your future, your family, and the generations that follow.

It's about becoming the architect of your next chapter — not a passive participant, not a bystander.

You have the power to design what comes next.

This book will help you do exactly that.

The Wealth Management Industry Is Built on Assumptions

If you've spent any time working with traditional financial advisors, you've likely noticed something: the wealth management industry is built on assumptions. Assumptions about what people need. Assumptions about what success looks like. Assumptions about what advice works. But if you're holding this book, you already know — those assumptions weren't made for you.

Most wealth advice is crafted for the mass affluent. For the "high-net-worth" individual — those measuring wealth in single-digit millions, not tens or hundreds of millions. Most advice is aimed at people climbing the ladder, not those already at the top. And certainly not those with concentrated positions in a single stock — an entirely different level of risk, opportunity, and complexity.

At the ultra affluent level, especially when your wealth is concentrated, most traditional advice doesn't just feel off — it collapses entirely. Here's why.

Cookie-Cutter Strategies Fall Apart

Most financial planning relies on off-the-shelf models. Simple asset allocation grids. Monte Carlo simulations designed to predict probabilities. Rule-of-thumb calculators for safe withdrawal rates. These tools work well when a client's financial world is simple: a 401(k), some mutual funds, a primary residence, and perhaps a few insurance policies. They're built for scale — to handle the middle of the bell curve efficiently.

But what happens when your reality doesn't fit that mold? When your balance sheet holds a concentrated position in a public or private company? When your wealth rides not on market beta, but on the success or volatility of a single asset? What happens when you're managing restricted stock, option grants, or a complex equity structure — not just a portfolio of ETFs?

Cookie-cutter advice can't handle this. These models weren't designed for your kind of risk. They weren't built for portfolios dominated by one position, for equity that might be illiquid for years, or for the intricate tax and liquidity questions that follow. You don't need rules of thumb. You need a strategy — custom-built, stress-tested, and tailored to your concentrated risk profile.

Most Advisors Aren't Trained for This

Here's another uncomfortable truth: most advisors aren't trained to deal with complexity at this level. They're good — sometimes great — at helping people get to $1 million, maybe $10 million. They know how to optimize a retirement portfolio, structure a basic estate plan, or diversify a standard set of mutual funds. But when it comes to concentrated stock, restricted securities, 10b5-1 plans, hedging strategies, and structured liquidity events? Most aren't prepared.

They aren't trained to help you unwind positions in a tax-efficient way. They aren't fluent in the nuances of hedging with collars, prepaid forwards, or charitable remainder trusts. They're not equipped to advise on strategies like exchange funds, derivatives overlays, or liquidity modeling post-exit.

And it's not just about technical skill — it's about mindset. At your level, you're not simply managing a portfolio; you're managing risk, reputation, opportunity, and legacy — all at once. You're solving for a different equation. You need advisors who can think beyond diversification clichés and see the full chessboard: tax law, estate planning, philanthropic vehicles, corporate governance, and generational transition.

Sophistication Without Complexity

A myth persists that wealth — especially concentrated wealth — must equal complexity. That the more sophisticated your financial life becomes, the more tangled it must be. More LLCs. More family limited partnerships. More offshore trusts. More legal entities and advisor silos.

But sophistication isn't about complication. Sophistication is clarity on the far side of complexity.

True sophistication means creating a financial life that is powerful, elegant, and coordinated. It means designing structures that aren't just tax-efficient, but understandable to you and the people who will inherit them. It's not about how many layers of protection you have — it's about how well those layers integrate, communicate, and flex as your needs evolve.

When you're unwinding a concentrated position, sophistication looks like a carefully architected exit strategy — one that balances tax mitigation, risk reduction, liquidity, and legacy without burdening you with a system so opaque that even your closest advisors can't explain it clearly.

An Architect, Not an Assembly Line

Think of your wealth like a custom-built home. You wouldn't hire a builder who mass-produces cookie-cutter houses. You'd hire an architect — someone who considers your family's needs, your tastes, your lifestyle, and designs something enduring. Your wealth deserves the same.

Unwinding a concentrated stock position isn't an assembly-line process. It's an architectural project. It requires design thinking — considering not just the tax implications of selling, but the emotional implications of shifting from high-conviction ownership to diversified stewardship. It means stress-testing liquidity plans against market downturns. It means layering risk management and philanthropy in ways that align with your life's mission, not just your tax bracket.

Why This Matters

When traditional advice fails you, it's not your fault. It's the model's fault. You've outgrown the frameworks that serve the masses. You've entered a world where the complexity of your position demands a different caliber of advice — advice that sees not just the asset, but the person behind it. Advice that treats your wealth not just as a portfolio to manage, but as a legacy to steward.

You need a blueprint — not for "more," but for better. Better strategy. Better governance. Better architecture. Better alignment between your wealth and your life.

Because unwinding concentrated stock isn't just about minimizing risk. It's about maximizing the freedom, flexibility, and impact your wealth was always meant to deliver.

Pros and Cons of Bespoke Wealth Management

Pros:

- Customized strategies tailored to your specific concentration risk and life goals.
- Integrated planning across liquidity, tax, investment, estate, and philanthropy.
- Greater alignment between your financial structure and your long-term mission.
- Clarity and confidence in decision-making.

Cons:

- Finding true experts takes time — not all advisors are equipped.
- Requires coordination across disciplines — legal, tax, investment — to succeed.
- Upfront complexity before achieving long-term simplicity.

- Higher professional fees for real expertise — but with proportionally greater value.

Action Steps

1. **Audit Your Advisory Team:** Are your advisors giving you mass-market advice or bespoke, integrated strategies? Are they capable of navigating concentrated stock risks and opportunities?
2. **Evaluate Your Current Plan:** Is your concentrated stock position being managed proactively — or ignored because it's too complicated?
3. **Set a 90-Day Goal:** Align your team and your strategy. Complexity unmanaged becomes a burden. Complexity intentionally architected becomes a powerful advantage.
4. **Demand Integration:** Tax, estate, investment, and liquidity planning must be orchestrated together. Silos create risk.
5. **Define Success Beyond Wealth:** What do you want your wealth — and your life — to achieve in the next decade? Let that vision guide your strategy.

Real-Life Scenarios

Case Study #1: A founder transitioned from standard wealth management to a custom wealth architecture. What was once a chaotic mix of advisors and strategies became an integrated system: tax, estate, investment, philanthropy — all aligned, coordinated, and centered around his family's vision. His concentrated position was unwound methodically, preserving wealth and minimizing tax exposure.

Case Study #2: Another founder ignored the concentrated stock risk for too long. When market volatility struck, over 40% of his wealth evaporated in a matter of months. The cost of "keeping it simple" was generational wealth lost — not because he lacked intelligence, but because he lacked a tailored strategy.

You didn't build your wealth through luck or accident. You built it with vision, discipline, and sacrifice.

Now it's time to steward it the same way.

You've outgrown mass-market advice. You deserve frameworks that respect your complexity and honor your aspirations. Because true wealth isn't about what you accumulate. It's about what you build, what you protect, and what you pass forward.

Ultra wealth deserves ultra wisdom.

Ultra Affluence Demands More Than Just Good Investments

If you're holding this book, you already understand something most people never will: wealth at the ultra-affluent level is not merely about the size of the balance sheet. It's about the architecture behind it. It's not about having more investments — it's about having more mastery. If you hold a concentrated position — a single stock, a single company, a single asset that dwarfs the rest of your portfolio — you don't just have wealth. You have a ticking clock.

You've outgrown simple diversification charts and basic tax planning. Ultra affluence demands a higher discipline — not just of growth, but of protection. Not just of success, but of permanence. This isn't about incremental gains. It's about structural clarity. It's about creating the kind of wealth framework that can outlast markets, cycles, and even generations.

This book is your blueprint for dismantling the silent risk of concentration and building something durable, scalable, and generational. Here's what you're going to build.

Building Your Wealth Command Center

If you're still managing your assets with scattered brokerage accounts, tax documents in separate folders, and a vague idea of how it all ties together, you're not managing your wealth — you're reacting to it. Winging it is not a strategy. It's a liability.

You need a system — a centralized Wealth Command Center — that pulls together every piece of your financial picture. Not just your investments, but your equity holdings, stock options, restricted shares, trusts, real estate, private investments, tax exposures, and liquidity pathways.

Think of it like the dashboard of a plane. At 30,000 feet and 600 mph, you can't afford guesswork. You need visibility. Precision. Real-time intelligence. Your command center becomes the nerve center of your entire wealth strategy, moving you from reactive wealth management to proactive wealth leadership.

Action Step: Audit your financial dashboard. Is your concentrated position integrated into your broader planning tools — or is it an afterthought? You can't manage what you can't see. Start there.

Creating Liquidity Without Losing Growth

The blessing and the curse of concentrated wealth: you look rich on paper, but liquidity is elusive. Shares you can't sell without crashing your own stock price. Options tied to vesting schedules. Restricted shares tied to company milestones.

Without liquidity, you lose optionality. Without optionality, you lose control.

Wealth mastery demands a liquidity strategy that doesn't force you to sacrifice growth. This means pre-arranged 10b5-1 plans, strategic use of structured sales, borrowing against diversified assets rather than liquidating prematurely, or using private lending markets to unlock liquidity discreetly.

Real-Life Scenario: A founder sat on a nine-figure equity stake for years, afraid to trigger a taxable event. When market conditions shifted, half his paper wealth disappeared. Compare that to a peer who steadily built liquidity over time — hedging, collaring, diversifying — and capitalized on market opportunities without panic.

Action Step: Map your liquidity horizon. How quickly could you unlock cash without cratering value or paying unnecessary tax? If you don't know, it's time to find out.

Managing Risk Like a Billionaire

Most people think insurance policies and a diversified 401(k) plan manage risk. Ultra affluence — especially with concentrated assets — demands far more. Your name, your reputation, your business interests — all are visible, and all are targets.

Risk is not just portfolio volatility. It's litigation exposure. It's tax law changes. It's reputational attacks. It's divorce, death, or market dislocation.

Risk management for you means preemptive structures: irrevocable trusts, asset protection vehicles, structured liquidity, careful ownership titling. It means shielding your concentrated assets before they ever become a liability. Defense doesn't happen after the threat — it happens before.

Action Step: Schedule a comprehensive risk audit. Not just insurance, but structure: trusts, entities, succession plans. Fortify before the storm, not after.

Mastering Advanced Investment Opportunities

Most investors never leave the shallow waters of public markets. You don't have that luxury. When your net worth is tied up in a single company or stock, you need uncorrelated, strategic investments elsewhere to offset that risk.

Private equity. Direct investments. Hedge fund strategies. Private credit. Real assets. Structured notes. But access doesn't equal advantage. Mastery means filtering opportunities ruthlessly. If you can't articulate how an investment fits your overall architecture — how it mitigates your concentration — it's not strategy. It's speculation.

Real-Life Scenario: One executive, flush with public company stock, threw capital into the next hot fund and watched it implode. Another, more disciplined, only invested where the alignment of interest and due diligence were ironclad — and built an alternative portfolio that offset single-stock volatility.

Action Step: Define your investment filter. What sectors, strategies, or managers earn your attention — and what criteria must they meet before you commit?

Structuring Generational Legacies and Philanthropic Plans

No one passes down a brokerage statement with pride. They pass down values. They pass down structures that endure.

Unwinding concentrated stock isn't just about selling and diversifying — it's about building frameworks that can endure the next liquidity event, the next market crash, the next generation's mistakes. Dynasty trusts. Purpose-driven foundations. Family constitutions. Governance councils.

Without structure, your estate becomes a legal free-for-all and your heirs become a cautionary tale. With structure, your wealth becomes a platform for generational leadership.

Action Step: Draft or revisit your family mission statement. If your wealth plan doesn't reflect your values, it's just a distribution schedule — not a legacy.

Curating an Elite Advisory Team Without Losing Control

Your lawyers, CPAs, investment advisors — they are not the pilots. You are. Too many ultra affluent individuals assemble an army of advisors without any generals — no coordination, no leadership, no accountability.

Curate your advisory board as you would a board of directors. Insist on collaboration, fiduciary alignment, and clarity. Dismantle silos. Hire slow, fire fast. Your legacy demands nothing less.

Action Step: Conduct an advisory audit. Are they integrated or isolated? Collaborative or competitive? If the left hand doesn't know what the right hand is doing, fix it — fast.

Why This Matters

This isn't about making you busier. You're busy enough. This is about giving you clarity. Control. Leadership.

You've already built wealth. Now it's time to master it. To transform a fragile, high-risk concentration into a stable, generational asset. To move from risk-taker to steward. From wealth accumulator to legacy architect.

Ultra affluence doesn't just give you more options — it gives you more responsibility. More at stake. More lives to impact. More history to shape.

Choose one action step from this chapter. One. Implement it before the month ends. Not tomorrow. Not someday. Now. Momentum is the ultimate antidote to complexity.

Because at this level, the difference between a paper fortune and a real dynasty isn't the size of your stock holdings.

Part I: The Foundation — Understanding the Challenge

Before you can solve a problem, you have to see it clearly. Part I lays the groundwork for everything that follows by exposing the hidden risks, emotional traps, and structural complexities that come with holding concentrated stock positions. It pulls back the curtain on the real dangers: not just market volatility or taxes, but inertia, overconfidence, and legacy risk.

We'll walk through why concentrated stock feels like an asset — but can act like a liability. We'll explore why so many highly successful individuals hesitate to unwind, even when diversification is the logical choice. And most importantly, we'll set the stage for strategic action by defining the stakes: the future of your wealth, your freedom, and your family's security.

This part doesn't offer quick fixes or platitudes. It forces the hard questions:

- What is the true risk of doing nothing?
- Why is concentration comfortable — but dangerous?
- What psychological biases are keeping you stuck?
- How can you shift from reactive ownership to proactive stewardship?

Through clear frameworks, real-world examples, and candid conversation, *The Foundation* equips you to move beyond complacency and into intentional action. Because you can't build a solution without first understanding the real scope of the problem.

Chapter 1: What Is Concentrated Stock and Why It's Dangerous

You didn't get here by accident. Whether you founded the company, joined early with a handful of stock options and a dream, or strategically accumulated shares over a lifetime of work, the concentration you now hold didn't just happen. It was earned — the result of focus, conviction, and discipline. In many ways, that concentrated stock position is the financial embodiment of your success. And that's why the conversation we're about to have can feel personal, even uncomfortable.

You see, wealth — real wealth — changes the game. It changes the risks you face, the opportunities you see, the complexity you have to navigate. And nowhere is that shift more dangerous, more misunderstood, than when it comes to concentration risk. In the early days, concentration was your ally. It's what multiplied your effort. Concentration in one company gave you exposure to upside that diversified portfolios couldn't match. In the early days, diversification would have been a drag on your trajectory. But now? Now, it's different.

Now, that concentrated stock position isn't just a source of potential. It's a source of exposure. A hidden risk, quietly compounding in the background while your portfolio value rises and falls with every market whim. Here's what's critical to understand: concentration builds wealth — but diversification protects it. What built your fortune is unlikely to preserve it.

Concentrated stock positions are deceptively dangerous. Not because they guarantee loss — but because they tie your financial fate to a single entity, a single market sector, a single management team, a single regulatory environment. The S&P 500, diversified across industries, sectors, and geographies, can recover from shocks. But one company? One company can miss earnings. One company can face regulatory backlash. One company can be disrupted by a new technology, a new competitor, a shift in consumer sentiment. Concentration means the margin for error narrows dramatically.

Real examples drive this home in ways numbers alone can't. Consider the former tech executive who watched, helpless, as his stock, once the darling of Wall Street, plummeted 80% during a sector downturn. His paper net worth — hundreds of millions — evaporated almost overnight. Not because the company was bad. But because markets are ruthless and indiscriminate. Or the founder who delayed diversification because of pride, belief, or fear — only to find herself locked out by insider restrictions and market declines when she finally decided to act.

At the ultra-affluent level, the stakes aren't just personal. They're generational. Your wealth is not merely about funding your lifestyle — it's about what it enables. Philanthropy. Legacy. Opportunity for your heirs. Freedom for you to choose what's next without being tethered to market volatility. Concentration threatens all of that.

It's not just the market risk you must consider. It's the liquidity trap. Wealth concentrated in a single company's stock is illiquid wealth. Sure, you can sell — but can you sell without moving the market? Without telegraphing signals you'd rather keep private? Without triggering tax consequences that slash the proceeds you actually keep? Liquidity is about more than access — it's about intelligent, efficient, strategic access. And concentrated stock positions often sit behind barriers of lock-up periods, blackout windows, and insider trading restrictions.

There's also the risk of timing. The illusion that "I'll sell when it's high" is a comfortable fantasy. But markets don't warn you before they correct. Companies don't send a polite note before bad news breaks. Timing risk — the risk that you'll be unable to exit at a time of your choosing — is one of the most underappreciated threats facing holders of concentrated positions.

And unlike broader market portfolios, where diversification spreads and mitigates this risk, concentrated stock leaves you naked to it.

Let's also confront the tax realities. The capital gains embedded in a concentrated position can be massive, the result of years — sometimes decades — of appreciation. Selling triggers those gains. And for many, that tax bill feels like a punishment for success. But waiting — doing nothing — only amplifies the risk that a market downturn will erase those gains before you can capture them. Sophisticated wealth management isn't about avoiding taxes. It's about managing them intelligently — using tools like 10b5-1 trading plans, exchange funds, charitable trusts, and staged selling strategies to reduce tax drag while methodically reducing exposure.

A founder I advised had a nine-figure position in his company after IPO. On paper, he was enviably rich. But emotionally, he was paralyzed. Selling felt like betrayal — of his team, his mission, his past self. He delayed. The stock dropped 60%. He didn't lose his fortune — but he lost flexibility. He lost options. He lost peace of mind. What he learned, painfully, was that concentrated wealth feels secure — until it isn't. Stewardship sometimes means making the hard, unglamorous, uncelebrated decision to protect, rather than chase.

And unwinding concentration doesn't have to mean abandoning your belief in the company. You can still be an advocate, a supporter, a shareholder — just a smarter one. A diversified one. One who's no longer betting your entire future on a single ticker symbol. There's a difference between loyalty and risk-blindness. True loyalty, to yourself and your family, demands intelligent action.

There are sophisticated strategies that allow you to unwind concentration without losing the upside you still believe in. Structured sales. Protective puts. Collar strategies. Exchange funds. Partial hedges. Charitable giving vehicles that align diversification with mission. The point is: you have options. But those options require planning. Precision. Professional guidance. They don't happen reactively. They happen proactively.

Why does this matter so much? Because wealth at your level is not static. It's dynamic. It's influential. Every dollar you protect, every risk you mitigate, every strategy you deploy — it's not just about balance sheets and tax returns. It's about freedom. The freedom to choose your next act. The freedom to pursue passion without pressure. The freedom to shape a legacy that's defined not by how much you accumulated, but by how wisely you stewarded it.

So if you find yourself wrestling with the idea of unwinding a concentrated position — if you feel the tension between loyalty and leadership — know this: you're not alone. Every ultra-affluent individual who's walked this path has faced it. And the ones who endure — who turn wealth into dynasty — are the ones who act.

I'll leave you with this: Wealth isn't about how high you can climb. It's about how well you can build once you arrive. Unwinding concentrated stock isn't about giving up. It's about stepping into your next role — from wealth creator to wealth architect.

It's time to ask: are you ready to move from exposure to security, from potential to permanence, from concentration to clarity? If you're ready, the next chapters will show you how.

Chapter 2: The Psychology of Concentration — Overconfidence and Familiarity Bias

You've seen it happen to others. Maybe you've even watched it unfold quietly among your peers — brilliant founders, top executives, early employees who rode a rocket ship to unimaginable wealth, only to find themselves clinging to concentrated stock positions long past when logic would dictate otherwise. Not because they lacked intelligence. Not because they didn't have access to world-class advice. But because of something subtler, more powerful: human psychology. And if we're being honest, it's not just their story — it's a temptation that comes for all of us who have built wealth in concentrated ways.

Let's start here: the very qualities that made you successful — conviction, deep knowledge, and relentless belief in what you built — are the same forces that now work against you. Overconfidence isn't arrogance; it's the inevitable byproduct of proximity and achievement. You know your company better than anyone. You lived through its risks, its battles, its reinventions. You've seen it outperform skeptics, analysts, and competitors. So when people talk about diversification, it feels almost… insulting. As if the standard rules of risk management should apply to someone else — someone who didn't have your insight, your access, your history.

But here's the trap: familiarity breeds comfort, not certainty. The behavioral finance world calls it "familiarity bias." We feel safer with what we know. Familiar companies, familiar sectors, familiar teams — they lull us into a sense of security. Yet from a risk perspective, familiarity is not protection. It's camouflage. It disguises the fact that all companies, even great ones, are vulnerable to forces beyond any founder's control — regulatory shifts, market cycles, technological disruption, changing leadership, black swan events.

I once sat across from a founder who had 85% of his net worth tied up in his company's stock — a company he built, nurtured, and took public. His argument against selling was almost poetic: "I trust it more than I trust anything else." And yet, when we mapped the actual risks — sector exposure, customer concentration, competitive landscape, geopolitical risks — even he had to admit: trust was not the same as diversification. Trust could not insure against the unknown.

Overconfidence works similarly but with an even sharper edge. It whispers that the rules don't apply to you. That you will know when to get out. That you will time the market just right. That your insider knowledge will give you a head start before trouble hits. But the markets are ruthless teachers. They do not grant passes based on familiarity or accomplishment. Timing a clean exit from a concentrated position is not just difficult — it's rare. The data is unforgiving: concentrated positions, left unmanaged, expose even the most brilliant minds to catastrophic loss.

There's also the emotional entanglement. Concentrated stock, especially when it represents a company you helped build, feels different than other assets. It's not just equity — it's identity. Selling it feels like surrender. Like cutting ties with a version of yourself you're proud of. This is where rational financial strategy collides with emotional reality. And this is where many otherwise disciplined individuals make their most expensive mistakes — clinging to stock not because it's the right move financially, but because emotionally, it feels safe, familiar, and affirming.

But the purpose of wealth — real wealth — is freedom. Not just financial freedom, but emotional freedom. Freedom from anxiety about market swings. Freedom from the invisible risks that concentration buries in your portfolio. Freedom to use your wealth as a tool for impact, not a monument to past victories. And that freedom only comes from acknowledging, and then transcending, the psychological traps that concentration lays.

The solution is not to demonize your company or your stock. It's to treat it with the respect it deserves — to recognize that the very forces that built your wealth cannot be the same forces that preserve it. True stewardship demands objectivity. It demands that you build a strategy that honors your success without being handcuffed to it. It demands that you diversify not because you lack conviction, but because you have the wisdom to know that conviction is not a risk management strategy.

There are intelligent, strategic ways to unwind concentrated stock positions — methods that respect the tax consequences, that consider market impact, that align with your values and goals. Structured exit strategies, tax-optimized selling plans, exchange funds, hedging tools, charitable vehicles — all can be deployed to reduce risk without unnecessarily sacrificing upside. But none of those tools matter if you don't first overcome the psychological barriers.

I've seen the shift happen. I've watched founders move from reluctance to relief. From fear to freedom. One client, after years of hand-wringing, finally began a structured, tax-optimized exit plan that reduced his concentration from 90% to 40% over three years. He didn't stop believing in the company. He didn't walk away from his legacy. What he did do was liberate himself — and his family — from the unnecessary burden of single-stock risk. He turned a potential vulnerability into enduring strength.

This is the point where strategy meets wisdom. Where stewardship demands a different kind of courage — not the courage to build, but the courage to protect. To ensure that what you've created doesn't end with you. Because ultimately, unwinding concentrated stock isn't about reducing numbers on a spreadsheet. It's about increasing options, increasing resilience, increasing the certainty that your wealth will serve you and those you care about for generations to come.

So I'll leave you with this question — one that only you can answer: Are you ready to master not just the financial mechanics of your wealth, but the psychology that surrounds it? Are you ready to lead not just your company or your investments, but your own instincts?

Because wealth is not just a measurement. It's a mandate. And mastering it begins when you refuse to let familiarity and overconfidence make your most important financial decisions for you.

If you're ready to take that next step — not just in thought, but in action — now is the time to align with a team that understands both the strategy and the psychology of unwinding concentrated risk. Wealth is complex, but with the right architecture, it can be clear. And clarity, at this level, is not a luxury. It's a necessity.

Chapter 3: The Risk You Don't See – Single Stock Volatility

When you sit atop a sizable position in a single stock, it's easy to forget the quiet, unseen risk you're carrying every day. Especially when that stock has been good to you. Especially when you know the business inside and out. Especially when the ticker symbol feels more like a badge of honor than an investment. But here's the uncomfortable truth: markets don't care about your history. Volatility doesn't respect your loyalty. And risk—the real, deep, structural risk—lives in places most can't see until it's too late.

Most conversations about stock risk start and end with broad market volatility—headlines about the S&P 500's daily swings or the Nasdaq's quarterly trends. But when you hold concentrated stock, you're not just tied to the market's rhythms. You're tethered to the fortunes of one company. One board. One leadership team. One sector. One brand's reputation. And as history shows us, no matter how big, no matter how dominant, no company is immune.

You've likely seen this before. Founders who once led iconic companies only to watch their fortunes crumble when scandal, competition, or even plain old market cycles turned against them. Early employees whose paper millions evaporated when Wall Street's mood shifted. Executives who assumed their insider status would shield them from volatility's wrath. None of them saw it coming. Not because they weren't smart—because they underestimated single-stock volatility.

Single-stock volatility is different from market volatility. It's sharper. It's more sudden. And most dangerously, it's asymmetric. A diversified portfolio might drop 10% in a market correction. A single stock can drop 40% in a day—and it doesn't need your permission to do it. Bad earnings report? Regulatory investigation? Leadership scandal? New technology disrupts the moat you thought was impenetrable? The reasons are endless, but the outcome is the same: wealth built over decades can be halved in weeks.

One founder I worked with had amassed a fortune of over $200 million, nearly all in the stock of the tech company he helped scale. The company was a darling—until it wasn't. Competitive pressures mounted, growth slowed, and a surprise leadership resignation sent the stock into a tailspin. He watched helplessly as his net worth fell by $80 million in less than six months. His comment to me, months later, was haunting: "I thought if anything happened, I'd have time to react. I didn't."

That's the illusion. The idea that because you are close to the business, you'll see the risk coming early enough to act. But markets move faster than human reflexes. Faster than board decisions. Faster than legal disclosures. Volatility doesn't send advance warning emails. It arrives when it arrives, and if your wealth is tied too tightly to a single stock, there's no seatbelt strong enough to hold you in place.

This isn't about fear. It's about freedom. Freedom that comes from understanding that your wealth should not be a hostage to one set of risks, one boardroom, one earnings report. Managing single-stock risk doesn't mean losing faith in your company. It means expanding your future beyond it. It means giving yourself, your family, and your legacy resilience against the inevitable storms.

The most disciplined founders and executives I've worked with approach this with the same rigor they brought to building their companies. They build unwind strategies—structured selling programs that respect tax consequences and market impact. They use hedging strategies intelligently, like collars or prepaid variable forwards, to manage downside risk without prematurely exiting their position. Some employ exchange funds, contributing their shares into a pool of other concentrated positions to instantly diversify without triggering capital gains taxes. Others layer in charitable remainder trusts, turning tax liability into philanthropic leverage.

No strategy is perfect. Each comes with trade-offs—liquidity, complexity, time horizons, and costs. But doing nothing is also a choice. And it's often the most dangerous one.

Another founder, who took a methodical approach to diversifying a $100 million position over five years, shared the peace of mind it brought. "It wasn't about betting against my company," he said. "It was about betting on my future."

That's the real risk of single-stock concentration—the risk that the wealth you've built is less stable, less resilient, and less secure than it appears on the surface. And the real opportunity—the one sitting quietly on the other side of this conversation—is to design a strategy that honors what you've built while protecting what you still want to create.

So here's the question you must wrestle with: Are you willing to let your financial future ride on a single stock, no matter how familiar, no matter how beloved, no matter how successful it's been so far?

Or are you ready to trade overconfidence for strategy, familiarity for freedom, concentration for control?

If you are ready, the first step isn't complicated. It's a conversation. With your advisor. With your CPA. With your legal team. Build the unwind plan before volatility forces your hand. Because once the storm hits, it's too late to chart a new course.

Managing wealth at this level isn't just about growing it. It's about protecting it, guiding it, stewarding it. Concentrated stock isn't just a financial asset—it's a responsibility. A responsibility to your future, to your family, to your legacy.

Wealth isn't just about accumulation. It's about stewardship. And stewardship starts by seeing the risks the world can't—or won't—see for you.

When you first build wealth, the dream is simple: create value, watch it grow, and ride the success story. In those early days, the idea of volatility feels abstract, almost academic. When your net worth is a few hundred thousand or even a few million, fluctuations are tolerable—painful perhaps, but survivable. But when your wealth has expanded into the tens, hundreds of millions—when it sits concentrated in a single name—volatility becomes something entirely different. It shifts from a background irritation to an existential threat. And here's the reality: most people never see it coming.

You've already beaten odds that few ever do. You helped build, scale, or steer a company to success. And along the way, you accumulated equity—founder shares, stock options, RSUs. It's natural that this stock represents not just wealth, but identity. It's the embodiment of your time, your skill, your risk-taking, your leadership. It feels less like an asset and more like an extension of you.

That's what makes concentrated stock so uniquely dangerous. It hides risk under the veil of familiarity. It convinces even the sharpest minds that they're immune to the market's capriciousness. "I know this company better than Wall Street does," you think. "I've sat in the strategy sessions. I've recruited the team. I've seen the projections. I've built the product." All true. But none of it changes the fact that you're exposed, and that exposure compounds in ways traditional diversification would naturally dilute.

Single-stock volatility isn't just theoretical. It's historical, it's documented, and it's brutal. Look back across the landscape of great companies—household names that, at their peak, seemed invincible. GE, once the gold standard of American corporate excellence, fell from over $500 billion in market cap to barely a shadow of its former self. Nokia, once the king of mobile, couldn't withstand the smartphone revolution. Enron, hailed as a Wall Street darling, collapsed not just because of fraud, but because belief in its invulnerability masked systemic risk.

Closer to our own era, think about Meta, Netflix, Tesla, or Zoom. World-changing companies whose stocks swung wildly—in some cases dropping 60-70% in a year. Nothing fundamentally illegal happened. No malfeasance. Just the reality of markets, sentiment shifts, competitive threats, regulatory risks, leadership turnover, and unpredictable macro shocks.

Here's the unnerving part: if you had sat inside any of these companies at their peak—if you were an insider, an executive, a founder—you likely would have felt confident. You would have believed you had information asymmetry. You would have trusted your proximity to management, to the board, to the roadmap. And yet, when the downdraft came, it didn't ask if you were on the inside or outside. It simply took its toll.

A founder I once advised held nearly 85% of his net worth—close to $400 million—in the stock of the company he co-founded 15 years prior. For a long time, the concentration was a point of pride. Why diversify when the returns were this spectacular? Why hedge against your own success? Then came a product delay, a missed earnings quarter, and whispers of a better-funded competitor on the horizon. In less than 18 months, the company's valuation was halved. The founder's paper wealth shrank by nearly $200 million. No fraud. No disaster. Just the slow bleed of market doubt—a bleed made fatal by concentration.

Why does this happen? Single-stock volatility isn't random. Individual stocks are exposed to what finance professionals call "idiosyncratic risk"—the specific risks that impact a company independently of the broader market. Unlike diversified portfolios where risks offset one another, single-stock holdings are exposed to the full brunt of company-specific failures: regulatory action, competitive disruption, management turnover, litigation, market saturation, or simple shifts in consumer behavior.

Consider how different this is from holding the S&P 500. If one company in the S&P collapses, the index absorbs the shock—because it's one among 500. Your wealth isn't catastrophically tied to the fate of a single management team or board decision. But with a concentrated position? It's binary. You ride or you fall.

To make matters more complex, concentrated stock is often illiquid. Not because you can't technically sell it, but because large sales can move the market—or trigger attention you might prefer to avoid. For insiders, additional restrictions apply: lockup periods, insider trading windows, SEC filings. Selling is not as simple as logging into a brokerage account and clicking "sell." Liquidity becomes a negotiation—timing sales without spooking the market or violating disclosure obligations.

This is why the smartest founders and executives build gradual, strategic unwind plans. They design selling programs (10b5-1 plans, for instance) that allow them to liquidate methodically, without reacting emotionally to market moves. They explore hedging strategies, like equity collars, which limit downside without triggering an outright sale. They consider contributing shares to exchange funds—vehicles that allow holders of concentrated stock to pool their shares and receive a diversified basket of assets in return, deferring capital gains taxes.

Are these strategies perfect? No. Every option has trade-offs. Hedges come with costs. Structured sales programs require discipline. Exchange funds have lock-up periods and diversification constraints. But they're better than the alternative: standing still, unhedged, concentrated, and vulnerable.

Another founder I worked with built a systematic plan to unwind a $250 million stock position over five years. His reason was simple: "I didn't want to be the richest person in the poorhouse." By the end of his unwind, the stock had appreciated another 20%, and he was still heavily exposed. But when volatility finally returned, slashing the stock by 50%, his diversified portfolio barely flinched. His lifestyle, his philanthropy, his family's plans—all remained intact. He didn't dodge volatility. He managed around it.

The greatest mistake is assuming you'll see it coming. Markets move faster than insiders react. Information leaks, rumors swirl, algorithms trade headlines, and liquidity dries up long before you can marshal a response. A stock can lose half its value before you even get a call from your general counsel confirming it's safe to trade again. Waiting for "better timing" is almost always an excuse disguised as strategy.

The real strategy is leadership. Leadership of your wealth, your future, and your freedom. It's not about betraying the company you helped build. It's about building a life—and a legacy—that endures regardless of what the markets throw your way.

You've built something remarkable. But real mastery now is not just holding on to wealth. It's translating wealth into control. Into autonomy. Into stewardship. Into a future where volatility is an opportunity, not an existential threat.

So here's the call to action: Don't let familiarity breed complacency. Don't let loyalty masquerade as strategy. Don't wait for volatility to teach you the lesson you could learn today, on your own terms.

The first step is deceptively simple. A conversation. With an advisor who understands concentrated stock risk at your level. With a team that sees beyond quarterly returns to generational resilience.

Because at this stage, wealth isn't just about what you've built. It's about what you'll preserve. What you'll protect. What you'll pass on.

And that starts not when the storm hits, but long before—by seeing the risk most don't, and acting before it sees you.

Chapter 4: Why Highly Compensated Executives, Founders and Business Owners Struggle to Let Go

If you've built something from scratch—if you've fought through sleepless nights, relentless competition, and endless doubt—you already understand something most people never will. Your company, your stock, isn't just an asset on a balance sheet. It's part of your story. It's your fingerprint on the world. And that's why, when it comes time to step back, to unwind, to diversify, it feels less like a financial decision and more like an emotional amputation.

Many founders and business owners struggle to let go—not because they lack the intelligence to recognize risk or the sophistication to understand diversification. They struggle because letting go feels like betrayal. Selling the stock of the company you birthed and nurtured feels, in a way, like disowning a piece of yourself. This isn't merely a tax event or an asset allocation decision. It's the culmination of years, sometimes decades, of sacrifice, belief, and identity.

We have to be honest: Concentration is comfortable. Not because it's safe—it's not—but because it's familiar. You know this company. You know its leadership team, its culture, its roadmap. You've seen its highs and lows. You've shaped its destiny. That familiarity creates an illusion of control, a sense that you can anticipate what the market can't. It becomes emotionally harder to trust an outside portfolio of nameless, faceless investments than the company where your fingerprints are everywhere.

There's also the powerful allure of past success. That stock, that equity, made you wealthy. It worked. Maybe spectacularly so. And as humans, we're naturally conditioned to believe that what worked before will work again. The success reinforces the concentration. It validates your belief that you know better, that the risk is less risky for you. It feels almost counterintuitive to sell the very thing that built your fortune in the first place.

But here's the truth that experience teaches—success changes the game. The risk that was acceptable at $5 million of net worth becomes catastrophic at $500 million. What was once a calculated bet becomes an existential exposure. Wealth changes the rules, but it doesn't change human nature. Founders who ignore that shift risk everything they've built, not just for themselves, but for their families and their legacies.

I once sat across from a founder who had built a company from two employees to 2,000. His stock represented nearly 90% of his net worth—hundreds of millions of dollars. He was brilliant, strategic, visionary. But every time we discussed selling down even a small portion of his stock, he resisted. "What if I miss out on the next leg up?" he would say. "What if it doubles again?" And so he held. And he watched. And eventually, he watched as a shift in the market—one that was no fault of his leadership—cut his company's valuation in half. He didn't just lose money. He lost optionality. He lost the easy freedom to walk into his next chapter on his terms.

Contrast that with another client, a quietly successful founder in the healthcare space. She began unwinding years before her exit was even visible to outsiders. She didn't liquidate recklessly—she designed a disciplined plan. A percentage of each year's vesting went toward diversification. A pre-arranged 10b5-1 plan allowed for systematic selling without emotion clouding the decision. By the time she exited fully, she had secured her family's future many times over, diversified, tax-optimized, and ready to fund not just a retirement, but a foundation.

It's worth reflecting on the psychology at play here. Founders are used to control. They are used to betting on themselves. Unwinding a concentrated position feels like surrender. But it isn't. It's leadership of a different kind. It's realizing that the skills that built your company—risk-taking, concentration, persistence—are not the same skills that protect your wealth and your family after the exit.

There's also the simple reality of inertia. Once wealth becomes tangled in a single stock, the logistics of unwinding can feel overwhelming. There are tax implications to consider. Trading restrictions if you're an insider. SEC reporting obligations. Emotional conversations with employees or co-founders. The complexity becomes an excuse to defer. "I'll get to it next year." But next year brings new market risks, new tax laws, new uncertainties. And the stakes only get higher.

At some point, you have to choose: Do you want to be remembered as the founder who rode the company up and watched it crash—or the founder who translated entrepreneurial success into lasting, strategic wealth? Because the real goal isn't just protecting what you've built—it's expanding your impact, expanding your freedom, expanding the lives you touch through intelligent, deliberate stewardship.

This is why unwinding a concentrated stock position is more than a financial exercise. It's a personal evolution. It's the founder maturing into the steward. It's the business owner becoming the architect of legacy. It's not a betrayal of what you've built—it's an expansion of it. It's the recognition that your company's success is a chapter, not the whole book.

The real risk is not selling too early. It's holding too long. The regret founders and business owners express most often isn't that they diversified—it's that they didn't diversify soon enough. That they waited until volatility forced their hand, rather than acting from a place of strength and foresight.

So here's the quiet, steady challenge: Reflect on your real goals. Is it about riding the stock price as high as it can go—or is it about ensuring that your success outlasts market cycles, economic downturns, and personal milestones? Is it about ego—or legacy? About accumulation—or stewardship?

Start with a conversation. Quiet, thoughtful, strategic. Look at your position. Ask yourself: If this stock dropped 30%, 50%, tomorrow—what would that mean for the life I've built, the family I love, the causes I care about? What would it mean for the next chapter of my life, not just the last one?

Because at this level, wealth is not about the adrenaline of holding. It's about the wisdom of letting go—deliberately, strategically, elegantly. It's about moving from founder to steward. From builder to protector. From success to significance.

And that shift begins—not with a massive liquidation or a radical overhaul—but with a single decision: to lead your wealth as intentionally as you led your company.

Chapter 5: Financial Literacy 101: Risk, Return, and Diversification

Let's be honest: if you're reading this, you're not new to risk. You've stared it down a thousand different ways—quitting safe jobs, betting on ideas that seemed crazy to the rest of the world, pouring time and capital into ventures that had no guarantee of success. You've earned your seat here because you understand how to take risks that matter. And it worked. But here's the quiet shift many founders and early executives miss: the skills that build wealth are not always the same skills that preserve it. At some point, the game changes. Risk looks different. Return demands more discipline. And diversification—an idea you might have brushed past during the grind—suddenly moves from optional to essential.

Let's start by getting something clear: risk is not inherently bad. Risk is the price of opportunity. It's the engine of outsized returns. When you were building, you needed risk. Concentrated stock was a feature, not a bug. It aligned you with the growth of your company. It gave you the upside you deserved for the sweat you poured into the venture. But now, risk without management isn't a wealth-builder. It's a wealth-destroyer. Risk that is concentrated in a single stock is not the smart, asymmetric bet it once was—it's a blind spot. A vulnerability. A single point of failure that could unwind everything you've created.

The financial markets reward risk—but only the right kind, at the right size, in the right places. When we talk about return, most people focus only on upside: the gains, the growth, the exits. But professional investors—those who steward wealth across generations—know that return must always be seen in the context of risk. Two investments might deliver the same return, but the one with lower risk is objectively better. And the best investors are not chasing the highest returns; they are engineering the best risk-adjusted returns. They are playing a game where the real metric is resilience, not just reward.

This is where diversification steps onto the stage. And let's be clear: diversification is not about dilution. It's not about settling for "average" returns. It's about building an anti-fragile wealth structure. One that can withstand the volatility of markets, the randomness of global events, the inevitable disruptions that no amount of strategy can predict. Diversification spreads your risk across different assets, different industries, different geographies, even different time horizons. It's not designed to eliminate all risk—nothing can. It's designed to ensure that no single failure can crater your future.

Imagine for a moment a table with one leg. It can stand, but the balance is precarious. A gust of wind, a slight bump, and the whole thing collapses. Now imagine a table with four, six, eight legs. One leg can crack, and the table still stands. That's the simple, brutal power of diversification. Your concentrated stock position—the one you know intimately, the one that made you wealthy—is just one leg. And no matter how strong it seems today, no matter how much you believe in it, no matter how rosy the future looks, relying on a single leg is not a strategy. It's a gamble.

Let's talk about why unwinding a concentrated position feels so counterintuitive to founders and early employees. It's because you have what behavioral economists call "familiarity bias." You're naturally more comfortable with the thing you know best. You've seen the quarterly reports. You've sat in the strategy meetings. You understand the vision better than any analyst ever could. But familiarity is not the same as safety. In fact, it often blinds us to risk. It tempts us to underestimate the volatility and overestimate the resilience of a single company—even a great company.

And overconfidence? That's the twin sister of familiarity bias. If familiarity makes us comfortable, overconfidence makes us believe we have more control than we actually do. Maybe you think you'll know when to sell. Maybe you believe you'll see the warning signs before anyone else. But markets have a brutal way of humbling even the most informed insiders. Black swans don't send advance notice. And once a concentrated position starts to fall, it often falls fast and far—much faster than liquidity allows you to exit.

Here's where the real power of financial literacy comes in. When you understand risk, return, and diversification at a deeper level—not just as academic concepts, but as real-world disciplines—you move from reacting to leading. You stop thinking in terms of single bets and start thinking in terms of systems. You realize that unwinding concentration is not surrender. It's strategy. It's leadership. It's a deliberate shift from being a founder or early employee to being the architect of long-term wealth.

Consider this: a diversified portfolio doesn't just reduce risk. It increases the reliability of outcomes. It smooths the path. It gives you the freedom to say yes to the next opportunity without the fear that a market correction will derail your future. It gives you the stability to engage in philanthropy, to fund the next generation, to live on your terms. Concentration might have built the rocket. Diversification builds the landing gear.

The most successful founders I've worked with understand this shift. They view diversification not as the end of growth, but as the evolution of growth. They recognize that their stock's story—no matter how compelling—is only one chapter in a much larger book. And they make the quiet, disciplined choice to turn concentrated wealth into enduring freedom.

So here's the question to sit with: Is your current wealth strategy still aligned with your current life? Or are you still playing the old game, long after you've outgrown it? The market doesn't care about loyalty. It doesn't care how many years you've given to your company. It cares about probabilities, volatility, and uncertainty. And the market punishes concentration eventually—always.

The first move is not radical. It's not emotional. It's simple: understand what you own. Understand the risk you're carrying. Understand the return you actually need—not the return you fantasize about. And then, with clear eyes and steady hands, start building a structure that isn't just built to grow—but built to last.

Financial literacy at this level isn't about spreadsheets. It's about stewardship. It's about shifting your mindset from founder to fiduciary—not just for yourself, but for everyone who depends on you, now and in the future.

If you take nothing else from this chapter, take this: Wealth is not just a reward for past risks. It's a responsibility for future generations. Mastering risk, return, and diversification isn't optional. It's the foundation of that responsibility.

Now might be the right moment to ask yourself: Is it time to move from intuition to intention? From concentration to strategy? From risk-taking to risk mastery? And more importantly—are you ready to start leading your wealth with the same brilliance that once built your company?

Chapter 6: The Tax Implications of Holding Too Much Stock

Let's start with a truth you already know at some level: taxes are not a side issue. They are not something to think about after the big liquidity moment, after the IPO, or after the sale. Taxes are a central feature of wealth management at the ultra-high-net-worth level. When you have concentrated stock, they're not just a consideration — they're a constraint, a cost, and, if handled poorly, a colossal missed opportunity. The stakes are higher here because your margin for error is larger. A tax misstep on a $5 million concentrated position hurts. A tax misstep on a $50 million or $500 million position can derail generational plans.

When you're sitting on a large block of stock — whether from founding a company, joining as an early executive, or acquiring a stake through some other meaningful path — the gains are typically significant. And so are the embedded taxes. Selling triggers capital gains. Holding creates estate tax risks. Passing it to heirs? Welcome to the 40% estate tax conversation. The instinct to delay, to defer, to "wait until next year" feels natural. Why rush to pay a tax bill if you don't have to? But here's the nuance: delaying action can compound your risks — and the longer you wait, the fewer options you have.

Capital gains taxes are often the first and most obvious concern. Long-term capital gains are taxed at 20% federally for most ultra-affluent individuals, but factor in the 3.8% Net Investment Income Tax and add state taxes — especially if you're in a high-tax state like California or New York — and your effective rate can easily top 30%. If you have a $50 million position with $45 million in gains, a full liquidation could trigger taxes of $13 million or more. That's not a small number. But taxes, while expensive, are predictable. Market volatility is not. Concentration risk is not. And a sudden 30%, 40%, or 50% decline in your stock's value can erase far more wealth, permanently, than a calculated tax bill ever will.

Then there's the estate tax dimension. If you hold your concentrated stock until death, it may qualify for a step-up in basis — meaning your heirs could inherit it without the embedded capital gains liability. Sounds great, right? Except for two problems. First, the estate tax itself: estates above the exemption threshold (currently around $13 million per individual, but subject to political winds) are taxed at up to 40%. If your estate is heavily concentrated in a single stock and that stock dips posthumously before liquidation, your heirs could be stuck paying a massive estate tax on a valuation that no longer exists in the market. Second, relying solely on the step-up strategy puts you at the mercy of future tax policy. Exemptions could shrink. Step-up provisions could be repealed. Planning by waiting is not planning. It's hoping.

Real-world examples drive this home. I sat across from a founder who held $100 million in pre-IPO stock. Post-IPO, he hesitated to sell, citing tax concerns. Over the next two years, the stock slid 60% — and so did his net worth. Yes, he avoided the initial tax bill. But what he really avoided was locking in his gains when he had the chance. Conversely, another client, a quiet, methodical early executive at a different tech firm, executed a disciplined, multi-year selling strategy through a 10b5-1 plan. He paid substantial taxes — tens of millions. But he also built a diversified, resilient portfolio that now funds a family foundation, multi-generational trusts, and several mission-driven investments. Taxes weren't the enemy. Taxes were the cost of freedom.

Managing the tax implications of concentrated stock is not about finding a magic bullet. There isn't one. It's about layering strategies intelligently: staged sales through pre-set plans, charitable giving to offset gains, strategic relocations to more tax-favorable jurisdictions, donor-advised funds for philanthropic efficiency, and in some cases, structures like exchange funds or qualified opportunity zone investments. Each tool has pros and cons. Each must be evaluated in the context of your total picture — your liquidity needs, your legacy goals, your time horizon, and yes, your tolerance for volatility.

For example, donating appreciated stock to charity doesn't just generate a deduction — it also eliminates the embedded capital gain. Set up a donor-advised fund, fund it with high-gain stock, and now you have a vehicle for strategic, tax-efficient giving that extends your influence and impact. Or consider an exchange fund: by pooling your concentrated position with other investors' concentrated positions, you get diversification without an immediate tax hit. These strategies aren't one-size-fits-all. They're custom suits, not off-the-rack jackets.

The key insight I want you to walk away with is simple but powerful: tax exposure is not a reason to freeze. It's a reason to act strategically. Taxes are part of the game — not the obstacle to playing it well. Every day you delay unwinding a concentrated position because of tax concerns is another day you accept uncompensated risk. Taxes can be modeled. Risks, once realized, cannot be reversed.

And remember: the goal isn't just to minimize taxes. It's to maximize after-tax, risk-adjusted wealth. It's to build freedom — freedom to fund your next venture, freedom to build a family legacy, freedom to support the causes you believe in, freedom to live on your terms, not the market's.

This isn't just about math. It's about mindset. Smart founders and executives don't shy away from complexity — they seek clarity through it. They don't get paralyzed by the cost of action — they measure it against the cost of inaction. Taxes are the toll you pay to cross the bridge to diversification, resilience, and legacy. Don't let the fear of the toll trap you on the wrong side of the river.

So here's your quiet but important call to action: If you haven't yet modeled the tax consequences of various unwind strategies — partial sales, gifting, exchange funds, charitable vehicles — now is the time. Not tomorrow. Not next quarter. Because unwinding a concentrated position isn't about giving up on your company. It's about giving yourself — and your family — the freedom to define the next chapter without a single stock dictating the terms.

Final thought: Concentration built your wealth. Strategy will protect it. Stewardship will extend it. Taxes? They're just part of the cost of playing — and winning — at the next level.

Chapter 7: Liquidity, Why It Matters More Than You Think

When you've spent years—maybe decades—building a company or watching a stock's value multiply, liquidity often feels like a distant, almost secondary concept. After all, when your net worth is tied to a soaring equity position, you don't think about cash the way most people do. You think about value creation. Growth. Multiplication. Cash can feel like a relic of a bygone era of paycheck-to-paycheck living—something other people worry about. But here's the truth: when it comes to wealth management at the ultra-affluent level, liquidity isn't just important. It's essential. And not understanding why—early and clearly—is one of the biggest silent risks of a concentrated stock position.

Liquidity, at its core, is about optionality. It's the freedom to pivot when the market changes. The ability to fund opportunities—real estate, venture capital, private equity—without hesitation. It's the shield against the unforeseen: a business downturn, a personal health event, a family need, or even broader economic upheaval. Liquidity isn't just about having money to spend. It's about having money to move. And the brutal truth is, without liquidity, even the most impressive net worth can become a liability.

Let me tell you about a founder I worked with years ago. Brilliant, driven, had a mid-nine-figure net worth almost entirely concentrated in company stock. On paper, he was untouchable. But when a family member faced a sudden medical emergency that required tens of millions in liquidity to access specialized care, we quickly realized the trap he was in. His stock was locked up due to insider restrictions. No 10b5-1 plan was in place. Selling on short notice would have triggered market concerns and personal scrutiny. He had assets—he didn't have access. And in that moment, the distinction wasn't academic. It was life-altering.

Liquidity planning, especially when tied to concentrated stock, is about looking ahead—not just to what can go right, but to what might go wrong. It's about building structures: lines of credit secured by stock or other collateral, pre-scheduled selling programs, diversified pools of liquid investments, and even the use of asset-backed lending facilities. It's about ensuring that your wealth can move at the speed of your life.

But liquidity is not free. There are costs—financial, tax, and opportunity costs—to accessing it. Selling stock incurs taxes. Borrowing against it incurs interest and risk. Holding too much in cash or short-term assets can mean giving up potential returns. The art is in the balance: how much to keep liquid, how much to lock into long-term, higher-yielding investments. How much to risk, and how much to reserve.

One strategy we often discuss is what I call a "liquidity sleeve." It's a portion of your overall wealth intentionally kept in highly liquid, low-volatility assets. Not because those assets will make you rich—they won't—but because they'll prevent you from being forced to make bad decisions under duress. If your concentrated stock drops 30% and you need cash, you don't want to sell into weakness. If a generational opportunity arises—a once-in-a-lifetime investment or philanthropic project—you don't want to be stuck waiting for stock sale restrictions to lift or market conditions to improve.

Founders and early executives, in particular, struggle with this. You're used to thinking in terms of growth, of the long game. Liquidity feels defensive, almost timid. But the ultra-wealthy who endure, who build legacies, who navigate storms without losing their way—those are the ones who respect liquidity. They don't just chase returns. They protect resilience.

A real-world example: one client built an incredible business and exited with a nine-figure windfall. Instead of plowing it all back into private investments or real estate, we carved out 20% of his post-tax proceeds into highly liquid assets. Over the next five years, that liquidity allowed him to fund two new ventures without touching his core wealth, make strategic philanthropic gifts at opportune moments, and navigate a messy legal dispute without selling long-term holdings. Liquidity didn't make him more money—it made him more powerful.

And that's what liquidity really is: power. The power to act when others are paralyzed. The power to weather volatility without panic. The power to buy when assets are cheap and everyone else is scrambling for cash. In concentrated stock positions, liquidity transforms you from a passive holder of wealth into an active, agile steward of it.

The final point here is critical: liquidity strategy must be proactive, not reactive. It's something you build when times are good, when markets are friendly, when options are abundant. Waiting until you need liquidity is like waiting until the storm hits to start building the ark. By then, it's too late. Strategic liquidity planning isn't just a safety net. It's a competitive advantage.

So here's your action step: if you can't articulate your liquidity strategy right now—if you don't know how much of your wealth you can access in 24 hours, 30 days, 6 months without disruption—it's time for a review. It's time to move beyond the simple view of wealth as a static number and start thinking about wealth as a dynamic, living system. One that must be both productive and protected.

Liquidity doesn't diminish your wealth. It amplifies its utility. It's not a drag on performance—it's insurance against poor decisions. It's not a cost—it's an asset in its own right. Done right, it ensures that your concentrated stock, your broader wealth, and your legacy remain tools in your hands—not risks waiting to be realized.

The deeper truth is that unwinding concentrated stock isn't just about diversifying risk or managing taxes. It's about creating the freedom to act on your terms. Liquidity is what lets you say yes to the right opportunities and no to the wrong ones. It's what allows your wealth to serve you, not the other way around.

Final note: Mastery of wealth is not about controlling markets or outsmarting cycles. It's about controlling your response to them. And that starts, always, with liquidity.

Chapter 8: Understanding Public vs. Private Stock Liquidity Events

You're sitting on something significant. It's not just the financial value of your stock—whether in a still-private startup you helped build from scratch or a publicly traded company whose name now flashes across news tickers. It's the story behind it—the nights no one saw, the risks you took when the odds weren't in your favor. The equity you hold isn't just numbers; it's narrative. It's legacy. But the market doesn't care about that. What matters now is liquidity. And liquidity, as you may have already realized, behaves very differently depending on whether you're holding private or public stock.

Liquidity in public markets is deceptively simple. You log into your brokerage platform, click a button, and shares become cash—at least in theory. But when you're an insider, a significant shareholder, or an executive subject to trading windows and regulatory scrutiny, the process becomes more nuanced. Trading volumes, SEC reporting requirements, insider trading regulations, and market impact concerns can make what looks like a simple sale feel anything but simple. You might be bound by 10b5-1 plans—pre-set, rule-based trading schedules designed to avoid the appearance of trading on inside information. You might face lock-up periods after IPOs, where even if your shares are theoretically liquid, they are contractually frozen for months. Timing, tax implications, and optics all collide in ways the average retail investor never has to consider.

Private stock liquidity events, however, are an entirely different animal.

If you're holding pre-IPO equity—founders' shares, RSUs, options—you're dealing with an illiquid asset class. There's no open market. There's no easy exit. Your liquidity is tied to rare events: a company sale, a merger, an acquisition, or an IPO. And even then, there's the problem of market appetite. Secondary markets have grown more robust in recent years, but selling private shares often comes with steep discounts and strict buyer qualifications. Valuations are subjective, negotiations are opaque, and liquidity, while possible, is slow and uncertain.

The strategic challenges of liquidity are different depending on where you sit on that public-private divide. In public markets, the biggest enemy is often emotional—fear of missing out on future gains or anchoring to past high-water marks. Many executives find themselves paralyzed, thinking, "I can't sell now—it was worth 30% more six months ago." They hesitate, waiting for the price to recover, not realizing that waiting introduces concentration risk all over again. In private markets, the challenge is structural. There might simply be no exit available. You might not have a choice to liquidate even if you wanted to.

Real-world case studies illustrate this vividly. Take a founder of a tech company pre-IPO, who receives a secondary offer from a private equity firm to sell a portion of their holdings at a 20% discount to the latest valuation. The instinct is to wait, believing that the upcoming IPO will command a premium. But six months later, the market cools, the IPO window slams shut, and no exit materializes. Opportunity lost—not because of bad business performance, but because liquidity wasn't properly prioritized or planned for.

Contrast that with an executive at a newly public firm, bound by a 10b5-1 plan. Over the course of a year, her shares are gradually sold at an average price—not the peak price, not the lowest price, but a disciplined, unemotional average. When the market dips 40% a year later, she's diversified, liquid, and sitting on optionality, while peers who waited for a perfect moment are now trapped, hoping for a recovery.

Liquidity events are, fundamentally, about control. In public markets, you have more control—but only if you plan ahead, structure your trades wisely, and manage the optics and compliance. In private markets, control is harder to come by. You must work harder—develop relationships with secondary buyers, structure liquidity preference agreements, advocate for tender offers if you're a leader within the company, or simply plan your financial life around a longer, less certain liquidity horizon.

Taxes, too, complicate both scenarios. Public stock sales create clear taxable events—long-term capital gains if held for over a year, short-term gains if not. Private stock introduces additional complexity: QSBS (Qualified Small Business Stock) exclusions, 83(b) elections for early exercise options, and AMT (Alternative Minimum Tax) implications on ISO (Incentive Stock Option) exercises. Mismanaging the timing or structure of your liquidity event can lead to unnecessary tax drag—what could have been a 0% capital gain under QSBS could instead turn into a 23.8% hit if you sell too soon or don't structure your exit properly.

Liquidity isn't just a financial decision; it's a strategic one. It's not about selling everything at once or holding forever. It's about designing a plan—deciding in advance how much liquidity you need, when you need it, and what risks you're willing to accept along the way. It's about understanding the constraints of your stock—public or private—and then building a diversified, flexible framework around that reality.

The key is intentionality. Too many founders and executives operate reactively—they respond to IPO lock-up expirations, they sell when the board says it's okay, they act only when forced. True wealth stewardship at this level means proactive liquidity design. It means engaging in tender offers early, crafting 10b5-1 plans before you need them, and understanding the liquidity profile of your net worth with precision.

If you're holding concentrated stock—public or private—the time to plan is before the event, not after. Have a conversation with your advisors. Understand the structures available to you: secondary sales, staged sales post-IPO, direct listings, SPAC mergers, liquidity facilities. Know the tax landscape. Build your liquidity strategy intentionally, not incidentally.

Because here's the truth: liquidity isn't about cashing out. It's about freedom. The freedom to live on your terms. The freedom to seize new opportunities. The freedom to protect what you've built and steward it wisely into the next generation.

And freedom, once again, is the real goal.

Would you like me to build the next chapter around specific strategies for creating liquidity pre- and post-IPO without sacrificing control or incurring unnecessary taxes?

Chapter 9: Behavioral Finance Traps When Managing Concentrated Wealth

There's a quiet risk that follows success — not market volatility, not tax policy shifts, but the more insidious risk of our own minds. If you've built a company or have been part of one that scaled beyond your wildest expectations, you know that discipline, vision, and resilience got you here. But when it comes to concentrated stock, those same traits can sometimes turn into obstacles. Behavioral finance — the study of how emotion and psychology influence financial decisions — teaches us that even the smartest, most capable individuals are vulnerable to traps. And at the ultra-affluent level, the cost of these traps is magnified.

One of the most common is overconfidence. It's natural: you believed in the company before anyone else did. You've been right before — perhaps spectacularly so. You saw the potential when the rest of the market was skeptical. So when it comes to your concentrated holdings, it feels almost disloyal or foolish to reduce your exposure now. After all, isn't this just the next phase of growth? Isn't the company poised to double again? Maybe. But maybe not. The market doesn't care about loyalty. Concentrated positions reward early believers — and punish those who fail to recognize when risk and prudence demand a different approach.

Closely tied to overconfidence is familiarity bias. You know your company. You know the leadership team. You've sat in board meetings, read the product roadmaps, seen the financials. That familiarity feels like insight — but it can also be a blindfold. Studies show that investors consistently overweight the value of assets they feel they understand, even when that understanding is superficial or outdated. Just because you know the story doesn't mean you know the future. Concentration in what feels familiar can lull you into a false sense of security, making it harder to diversify when diversification is exactly what's called for.

Then there's anchoring — the mental trap of clinging to a specific price point. Maybe your stock hit $200 a share last year. Maybe it fell to $150. Selling at $150 feels like defeat — like locking in a loss against that psychological benchmark. You tell yourself, "I'll wait until it gets back to $200, then I'll sell." But markets are not obligated to revisit old highs. Anchoring to a prior valuation can cause paralysis, leading to inaction at precisely the time when action would protect and preserve your wealth.

Another subtle trap is the endowment effect — the tendency to assign more value to something simply because you own it. Behavioral studies show that people demand significantly more to give up an asset they own than they would pay to acquire it. In the context of concentrated stock, this effect can create a dangerous distortion. You see the stock as uniquely valuable, not just another holding. You value it for its history, its story, its connection to your career. But the market values it dispassionately. Ignoring that disconnect can leave you overexposed and underprotected.

Loss aversion also plays a role. Humans are wired to feel the pain of losses more acutely than the joy of equivalent gains. In financial terms, the fear of losing money leads people to hold onto risky positions longer than they should. You may rationalize that selling would crystallize a loss — but holding a concentrated position through another market cycle could crystallize something far worse: a permanent impairment of capital. Ultra-high-net-worth individuals often feel this even more acutely because the stakes are so much higher. Millions — sometimes tens or hundreds of millions — are on the line.

Confirmation bias can reinforce all of these traps. Once you've decided the company is a winner, you unconsciously filter out information that contradicts that belief. You seek out bullish analyst reports, positive news articles, and glowing endorsements from colleagues. You dismiss or downplay negative indicators. Left unchecked, confirmation bias creates an echo chamber around your investment thesis, narrowing your view when you need it to be widest.

I once sat with a founder who built an exceptional business — one that became a household name. When he first considered unwinding part of his stake, he was frozen by fear and second-guessing. "I know this company better than anyone," he said. "Selling feels like betting against myself." We reframed the conversation: "Selling isn't betting against yourself. It's betting on your future." Over the course of a year, he strategically reduced his concentration, diversified into a thoughtfully constructed portfolio, and positioned his family for multigenerational security — without giving up his belief in what he built.

The antidote to these behavioral traps isn't brute force. It's structure. It's systems. It's developing a pre-committed plan — perhaps a 10b5-1 trading plan if public, or a staged secondary sale strategy if private — that removes emotion from the equation. It's surrounding yourself with advisors who can provide dispassionate counsel, grounded in data and experience, not in emotional attachment. And it's about redefining success: not as holding on to the bitter end, but as stewarding the wealth you've created to enable freedom, security, and impact.

None of this is easy. If it were, you wouldn't need this conversation. The reality is that behavioral traps are powerful because they feel right in the moment. But wealth stewardship at this level demands a higher standard — one that acknowledges those feelings, respects them, and then moves beyond them toward disciplined, strategic action.

If you recognize any of these patterns in yourself, the call to action is simple: pause. Reflect. Begin designing a strategy that respects the emotions you feel but isn't governed by them. Whether that means setting up a formal diversification plan, engaging a wealth advisor who specializes in concentrated wealth, or simply beginning with a liquidity analysis — the point is to start. Because the greatest risk isn't market volatility or tax changes. It's the silent, internal biases that keep you from making the strategic moves your future self will thank you for.

Managing concentrated stock isn't just about numbers on a spreadsheet. It's about mastering yourself — your instincts, your fears, your hopes. It's about trading emotional comfort for strategic clarity. And it's about building not just wealth, but freedom — the kind of freedom that comes from knowing you've moved past the traps and into true stewardship.

Let's build on where we left off. You've accepted the reality that concentration risk is not just theoretical — it's personal. You've come to terms with the behavioral traps that can silently sabotage even the most accomplished individuals. Now, the question is not *if* you should act, but *how* you should act.

At this level, selling is not as simple as logging into an account and clicking "sell." With significant positions — especially if you're an insider or subject to trading windows — you must move with strategy and precision. Liquidity must be created without disrupting markets, alarming shareholders, or running afoul of securities regulations. Fortunately, you have access to sophisticated tools that can help. Let's walk through them.

First, the 10b5-1 trading plan — the unsung hero of the public market insider. If you are still serving in an executive role, or if you hold insider information, you're subject to blackout periods and trading restrictions. You can't just sell stock whenever you feel like it. But a 10b5-1 plan provides a compliant path forward. Essentially, it's a pre-set, SEC-sanctioned plan that allows you to sell a predetermined amount of stock at predetermined times or price points, irrespective of what you know later. It provides two critical benefits: it gives you legal protection against insider trading claims, and just as importantly, it forces discipline.

The real beauty of a 10b5-1 plan is emotional. It liberates you from market timing temptation. Once the plan is set, the trades execute automatically. You're free to focus on what you do best — building companies, mentoring leaders, investing in innovation — without the emotional noise of monitoring stock prices daily. I once worked with a founder who hesitated to set up a 10b5-1 because he feared losing control. Six months later, with a volatile market swinging wildly, he admitted that the plan saved him from his own instincts — executing steady sales even while headlines screamed panic.

But what if your stock is still private? That's where secondary markets come into play. Private secondary markets have matured significantly over the last decade. Platforms now exist that specialize in connecting founders, early employees, and investors with buyers — family offices, institutional investors, even specialized secondary funds — looking to acquire private shares. Done well, these transactions can unlock liquidity at fair valuations without the need for a full company exit.

Navigating the secondary market, however, is delicate. Every transaction must consider valuation, company approval rights, right of first refusal clauses, and the message that selling sends to the broader investor and employee base. You'll want advisors who know how to position the sale discreetly and structure terms that align with your broader liquidity and tax strategy. Done poorly, secondary sales can signal insider doubt. Done well, they are just prudent stewardship of personal balance sheets.

For many, the answer isn't a single plan but a staged liquidation strategy. It's about blending tools — a little bit of 10b5-1 execution, a little bit of secondary liquidity, and strategic liquidity events like tender offers, cash-outs during new funding rounds, or post-IPO dribble sales under Rule 144. This approach respects market realities, tax optimization, and your personal need for freedom without sending disruptive signals to markets or partners.

Tax efficiency must also be layered into the plan. Selling concentrated stock can trigger enormous capital gains taxes if done without foresight. Strategies like donating appreciated shares to donor-advised funds for philanthropic goals, or timing sales to align with other taxable events (such as offsetting realized losses elsewhere in your portfolio) can make a significant difference in after-tax proceeds. Even better, when secondary sales are structured thoughtfully, you might be able to utilize QSBS (Qualified Small Business Stock) exemptions or carefully choreograph gains into lower-tax years.

Liquidity planning, too, must address more than just immediate cash needs. It should position you to capitalize on future opportunities. Once free from the psychological grip of concentration, your capital can go to work in diversified portfolios, private investments, direct deals, and strategic philanthropy — all aligned with your long-term vision, not just your short-term liquidity.

A real-world example: one founder we worked with had 80% of her net worth tied up in a company she adored — but she also wanted to invest in climate tech funds and start a private foundation. Through a blend of 10b5-1 sales post-IPO, structured secondary sales negotiated pre-IPO, and well-timed charitable stock donations, she was able to systematically unlock liquidity without destabilizing her company, and without a heavy tax hit. Today, she's both an investor and a philanthropist, using her freed-up wealth to amplify her second act — with far less stress than when she was overexposed.

The real win here isn't just unlocking liquidity. It's unlocking freedom. Freedom from single-company risk. Freedom to invest according to your values and vision. Freedom to build a more dynamic and resilient financial life — one not bound to a single ticker symbol.

As you think about your next move, ask yourself: are you managing your wealth for the next quarter or for the next generation? Are you trapped in your company's story, or are you ready to start writing the next chapter of your own?

Now is the time to sketch out your unwinding strategy — not in a rush, but with intentionality. Start with a conversation: with a wealth advisor who understands concentrated stock, a tax strategist who sees beyond April 15, a legal expert who can structure compliance and governance intelligently.

Because at this level, wealth isn't just a number. It's a responsibility. And how you unwind concentration will say as much about your stewardship as how you built it in the first place.

When you reach the point where your stock has created transformative wealth — but also created oversized risk — it's time to graduate from basic strategies to more sophisticated tools. Because here's the truth: selling isn't always the ideal first move. Sometimes you need protection *before* you need liquidation. And that's where advanced hedging comes in.

You see, most conversations around concentrated stock start and end with "just sell some." It's simple advice — but oversimplified for someone like you. What if you can't sell due to lockups or insider restrictions? What if you *shouldn't* sell yet because of tax reasons or strategic timing around market events? What if selling now would disrupt voting rights, signal weakness, or cap your upside prematurely?

Sophisticated wealth stewardship demands more tools. You don't just need liquidity — you need control. You need a plan that manages downside risk without giving up all your upside. You need strategies that allow you to defer taxes and align your liquidity with your long-term objectives. Let's walk through a few of the most powerful tools available.

The first — and arguably simplest — is the **collar**. In essence, a collar strategy sets a floor and a ceiling on your stock. You buy a protective put option, giving you the right to sell your stock at a predetermined price (the floor), and you sell a call option, agreeing to sell your stock if it rises above a certain price (the ceiling). The beauty? The premium you receive for selling the call can often offset — or even fully pay for — the protective put. In practice, this creates a defined range of outcomes for your stock: you limit your downside while capping your upside.

For founders or executives nervous about volatility but not yet ready to liquidate, collars can be a lifesaver. One founder I advised had nearly $100 million in concentrated tech stock — but was in the middle of an important lock-up. A collar allowed him to sleep at night, knowing that if the stock plummeted, his downside was capped — and if the stock soared, well, he had agreed to cap his upside, but still locked in a life-changing amount.

Next, let's talk about the **prepaid forward contract** — a more sophisticated, but incredibly flexible tool. A prepaid forward is essentially a deal where you agree to deliver your shares at a future date, but receive a substantial portion of the proceeds up front — typically around 75-90% of the current market value. Structurally, it's not a sale in the eyes of the IRS at the time of execution, meaning you defer realizing capital gains until the shares are actually delivered years later.

Prepaid forwards provide instant liquidity without triggering immediate taxes. You can use the proceeds to diversify, invest, fund ventures — all without the tax drag of an outright sale. Better yet, many prepaid forwards are structured with floors and caps, similar to collars, allowing you to protect your downside while sharing in some upside growth. If timed well — particularly in periods of high share valuation — it's an elegant way to both hedge and access liquidity without losing the strategic positioning of your stock.

Now, what if you want diversification without selling at all? Enter **exchange funds** — one of the more underutilized but potent tools for concentrated wealth. Exchange funds allow you to pool your shares with those of other investors in similar situations. Imagine a fund where executives from tech, healthcare, energy, and finance companies all contribute their concentrated positions. In return, each participant gets shares in the diversified fund — not a direct sale of their stock.

Exchange funds are particularly valuable for patient capital — individuals who don't need immediate liquidity, but who recognize the long-term peril of being overweight a single stock. Because there's no sale, there's no immediate capital gains tax. You defer taxes until you eventually sell the diversified fund interests. The trade-off? These funds often have lock-up periods — typically seven years or more — and your liquidity will be dictated by the fund's terms, not your personal timetable. But for those committed to long-term diversification, the benefits can be profound.

There's another nuance worth mentioning here. Many hedging strategies — collars, prepaid forwards, even exchange funds — are viewed favorably for *planning around estate and gifting strategies.* You can transfer hedged positions into trusts more efficiently because the risk-mitigation lowers the valuation, reducing the taxable gift value. In estate planning, that can translate to millions in transfer tax savings.

Yet, none of these strategies are "set and forget." They require sophisticated structuring. You must navigate insider trading restrictions, ensure compliance with Rule 144 and 10b5-1 planning, negotiate favorable terms with financial counterparties, and monitor collateral requirements and margin maintenance over time. Poorly executed, these strategies can create tax surprises, liquidity squeezes, or even worse — margin calls at the worst possible time. Well executed, they provide the insulation and flexibility you need to transition from high-concentration to high-stewardship wealth.

One client story illustrates this vividly. She was an early executive at a high-flying tech company and sat on a $200 million block of stock. She didn't want to sell during volatile markets — but she couldn't afford to lose half her wealth to a bad quarter. Using a combination of a prepaid forward for liquidity, a collar for downside protection on the remaining stock, and careful exchange fund diversification, she moved methodically over five years from 90% concentration to 30% — without triggering premature taxes or sacrificing upside. Today, she has a diversified balance sheet, a robust philanthropic plan, and a family governance structure in place — none of which would have been possible if she had stayed paralyzed by indecision.

These tools — collars, prepaid forwards, exchange funds — they're not just finance toys. They're freedom tools. They allow you to design a financial architecture that reduces risk, increases flexibility, and preserves opportunity. They are the bridge between your current concentrated risk and the diversified wealth that will support your next act — whether that's launching a venture fund, starting a foundation, mentoring startups, or simply living a quieter, freer life.

As we close this chapter, here's your real question: Are you building your wealth to withstand a bad market day, or are you building it to sustain a century? Because at the ultra-affluent level, the goal isn't just protection — it's durability. Resilience. Stewardship.

Start by asking your advisors — are we thinking beyond sales? Are we exploring strategic hedging? Are we coordinating across tax, legal, and investment lenses? Because if you're not — you're not truly protecting what you've built.

Chapter 10: Case Studies, Founders, Business Owners, and Highly Compensated Employees Who Got It Right (and Wrong)

There's something powerful about learning through real-world experience — especially when that experience belongs to someone else. You've built your success by understanding nuance, by seeing patterns that others miss. In the world of concentrated stock, the difference between protecting a fortune and watching it evaporate often comes down to strategy — or the lack of it. Let's walk through a few real-life case studies. You'll see not only the mechanics of good planning, but also the human instincts — sometimes brilliant, sometimes fatal — that drive decision-making at the highest levels of wealth.

Take David, a founder of a SaaS company that became a market darling seemingly overnight. After the IPO, David found himself holding $150 million worth of company stock, almost all his net worth tied to one ticker symbol. He was loyal to the mission, proud of what they had built, and believed deeply in the company's future. But David was also pragmatic. He understood that markets don't move in straight lines and that founders are often the last to see storm clouds. Working with his advisory team, he implemented a 10b5-1 plan — a pre-scheduled, SEC-compliant selling strategy — locking in regular liquidity over a 24-month period.

David didn't try to time the market. He didn't chase the peak. Instead, he diversified systematically. By the end of the program, he had reduced his single-stock exposure to under 30% of his net worth, built a diversified portfolio, and seeded a family foundation. When a surprise earnings miss cut the stock's value in half, David's fortune was bruised but not broken. His financial freedom — and the future he envisioned for his family — remained intact.

Contrast David with Mark. Mark was an early executive at a well-known biotech company. He had spent two decades climbing the ranks and had accumulated $80 million in stock options and RSUs. Mark believed — fervently — that his insider knowledge gave him an edge. He ignored every advisor's suggestion to diversify. Why sell now? he reasoned. The real upside was just around the corner.

Then came the bad news. A failed Phase III drug trial sent the company's stock into freefall. In less than six months, Mark's $80 million paper fortune was worth less than $10 million. Worse, he had already exercised many of his options — triggering AMT (Alternative Minimum Tax) liabilities based on their peak value. The stock's collapse left him facing tax bills on gains that had, in reality, disappeared.

The lesson? Mark's downfall wasn't ignorance — it was overconfidence. He trusted his familiarity with the company more than he respected market risk. And he paid the price for it.

Now, consider Sarah, a highly compensated employee at a tech giant known for its generous equity grants. Over years, her RSUs accumulated into a $30 million position — concentrated entirely in her employer's stock. But Sarah was thoughtful. She recognized that her human capital (her career) and her financial capital were both tied to the same company. If the company faltered, she'd be vulnerable two ways: her income and her wealth would both take a hit.

Sarah built a diversification plan over five years, using restricted stock sales combined with strategic reinvestment into diversified portfolios and real estate. She avoided the temptation to move all at once — which would have been tax-inefficient. Instead, she worked with her CPA and wealth advisor to layer her sales, managing her tax brackets and using charitable contributions to offset gains. When her employer hit a rough patch and the stock slid 40%, Sarah's portfolio remained resilient. Her financial life wasn't defined by the fortunes of a single company.

On the other side, there's Jessica — another tech executive, another concentration story. Jessica was proud of her wealth, and rightly so. She had been there since Series B and had earned every penny of her $50 million in stock. But she couldn't bear the thought of selling — even a little. To her, selling felt like betrayal — like signaling to the world that she didn't believe in the company. And so, she held on. Through good news, bad news, volatility, market crashes. She held on because she believed.

Jessica's loyalty was admirable. But markets don't reward loyalty — they reward strategy. When a broader tech market correction hit, her $50 million shrank to $22 million. Still life-changing money, yes. But it was avoidable. Her mistake wasn't in believing in the company — it was in failing to separate belief from financial prudence.

If there's a common thread across all these stories, it's this: Emotion is the enemy of wealth stewardship. Overconfidence, loyalty, familiarity — they're human. They're understandable. But left unchecked, they're dangerous. Financial literacy at the ultra-affluent level isn't about knowing how to pick stocks. It's about knowing how to manage risk. It's about knowing when to step back, look at your wealth objectively, and make decisions rooted in logic, not loyalty.

The founders, business owners, and executives who get it right don't view unwinding their concentrated stock as an abandonment of their vision. They see it as a continuation of it — ensuring that the success they built isn't vulnerable to the whims of a single stock chart. They build liquidity thoughtfully. They hedge risk strategically. They act with discipline, not emotion.

As you sit with your own concentrated position — whether it's $10 million, $100 million, or more — the real question is not, "Should I believe in my company?" Of course you should. The question is, "Should my financial future rely entirely on it?" Because at this level, wealth is about more than belief. It's about stewardship. It's about designing a financial life that honors what you built — and protects it for decades, even generations, to come.

The call to action is simple but not easy: Don't let loyalty, pride, or fear trap you in concentration risk. Assemble your team — your wealth advisor, your CPA, your legal counsel. Build your unwind strategy. Execute it with the same discipline and clarity that built your company in the first place. Wealth is not just about accumulation. It's about stewardship.

Part II: First Principles — Key Financial Literacy Concepts

Wealth at this level demands more than instinct and ambition — it requires mastery of the fundamentals. *Part II* is about grounding you in the key financial literacy principles that every ultra-affluent individual needs to not just protect, but intelligently grow and steward their fortune. These are not the basics you learned in business school or along your entrepreneurial journey. These are the deeper, more sophisticated truths about how capital works once you've already succeeded, when the stakes are higher and the margin for error smaller.

In these chapters, we explore foundational ideas: how risk really operates in concentrated stock positions, why diversification isn't about dilution but about durability, how liquidity is your hidden superpower, and how taxes — when managed intelligently — become a lever for preserving and multiplying wealth. We also dive into the behavioral traps even the smartest founders and executives fall prey to: overconfidence, familiarity bias, emotional attachment to stock, and the tendency to treat market swings like personal verdicts.

You will not find lectures here. You'll find conversations — precise, direct, and practical — built to replace outdated mental models with clarity and strategic sophistication. The goal is simple: to ensure you're not just wealthy on paper, but wealthy with purpose, with resilience, and with a plan. By the end of this section, you'll be equipped with the literacy to move beyond accumulation into the deeper, more durable work of true wealth stewardship.

Because financial freedom isn't just the absence of worry — it's the presence of intelligent, disciplined action. And that begins with mastering the principles most never take the time to learn.

Chapter 11: Asset Allocation, Your New Best Friend

When you've spent years, maybe decades, building wealth through the success of a single company, asset allocation can seem almost counterintuitive. After all, your success was built on focus — a massive, outsized bet on one entity, one mission, one idea. And that focus paid off. But the same strategy that built your wealth is not the strategy that will preserve it. In fact, continuing to concentrate your financial future in a single stock — no matter how beloved, no matter how successful — is playing a different game without updating your playbook. Asset allocation becomes the pivot — the quiet, powerful shift from building wealth to stewarding it.

Asset allocation is, at its core, the deliberate distribution of your wealth across different asset classes: equities, bonds, real estate, private investments, cash, and alternatives. But framing it as just a diversification tool would miss its true elegance. Asset allocation is not just about spreading bets; it's about building resilience. It's your best friend because it protects against the one risk you can't diversify away by holding on to concentrated stock: the risk that your future self needs flexibility, and a market event — outside your control — compromises it.

The volatility of single stock concentration is rarely visible day-to-day, especially when markets are good and the company is thriving. But history reminds us — painfully and consistently — that even the most dominant companies can falter. Think about once-unassailable giants like Kodak,

Nokia, or more recently, the sharp reversals seen in high-flying tech stocks. A diversified asset allocation isn't a hedge against success; it's a fortress against complacency and market whims. It ensures that one corporate misstep, regulatory shift, or economic downturn doesn't undo the years you spent building.

Now, you might be thinking, "But I know this company inside and out. I can spot the risks better than anyone." And that may be true — for now. Yet the nature of risk is that it often arrives from the outside, unannounced, in forms even insiders can't predict. It's not a lack of intelligence or effort that leads to concentrated wealth collapses. It's the false sense of security that familiarity breeds. Asset allocation is the antidote to that overconfidence. It's not about doubting your company — it's about respecting uncertainty.

A sound asset allocation strategy begins by assessing your total financial picture — not just your brokerage statement. What are your liquidity needs over the next five, ten, twenty years? What obligations, ambitions, and legacy goals need to be funded regardless of market conditions? What risk exposure are you truly comfortable with when viewed not through the lens of optimism, but through the harder lens of stewardship? These aren't investment questions. They are life questions. Asset allocation translates them into action.

Consider the real-world story of a founder who sold a large portion of her company at IPO but retained a significant position post-offering. She wisely worked with her advisory team to gradually build a balanced portfolio — public markets, private equity, municipal bonds, real estate, and a strategic cash reserve. When her company's stock faced an unexpected regulatory headwind, wiping out 40% of its value in under six months, her diversified allocation meant her net worth dipped only modestly. More importantly, her long-term goals — family philanthropy, private investments, a planned charitable foundation — remained fully on track. She didn't just survive the volatility; she thrived through it.

Contrast that with another executive who, believing fervently in his company's future, resisted every call to diversify. He rode the stock to its peak and watched helplessly as it plunged 70% after a market downturn.

The hit wasn't just financial; it was emotional. His identity was intertwined with the company's stock price. And when that collapsed, so did much of his sense of financial security. Asset allocation wouldn't have prevented the market cycle, but it would have softened the blow — giving him optionality and stability when he needed it most.

Asset allocation also has powerful tax implications. Managing gains, harvesting losses, timing capital distributions — all these strategies depend on having a range of assets to work with, not just a single concentrated position. A well-diversified portfolio gives you tools, levers to pull when liquidity is needed or when tax opportunities arise. Concentration leaves you boxed in, at the mercy of market timing and tax consequences you can't easily control.

And here's the real genius of allocation: it's dynamic. It evolves as you evolve. Early in the wealth cycle, you may need more growth assets. As you transition to legacy building, income generation and principal preservation take priority. Asset allocation adjusts — strategically, intentionally — to ensure your wealth strategy matches your life strategy. It's not static diversification. It's dynamic stewardship.

If you haven't yet built your asset allocation blueprint, consider starting today. Not with a generic model or an off-the-shelf portfolio, but with a plan engineered around you: your liquidity needs, your risk tolerance, your long-term goals, your legacy ambitions. Start by asking yourself: if my concentrated stock were to drop by 50% tomorrow, what would that mean for my financial future? How much of my wealth is truly exposed to a single outcome, and how comfortable am I with that exposure?

The action step is simple but profound: move from passive acceptance of concentration to active allocation. Build a system that ensures your future isn't held hostage by a single stock price. Engage a team — an advisor who understands the nuances of concentrated wealth, a CPA who can navigate tax complexities, a legal counsel who sees the estate planning angles. Asset allocation isn't about abandoning your company's story. It's about writing the next chapter on your terms — with more freedom, more stability, and more control.

Because at this level of wealth, resilience matters more than bravado. Optionality matters more than loyalty. And asset allocation? It's not just an investment tool. It's the quiet, steadfast architecture behind lasting legacy.

Chapter 12: Modern Portfolio Theory Simplified for Founders

Let's set the scene. You've spent years, maybe decades, building something rare — a company that defied the odds. You took risks that most people would never dream of, and they paid off. Today, your concentrated stock position stands as proof of that success. But if you're being honest, the more your wealth has grown, the more it feels like you're carrying a single, massive boulder uphill. And no one told you — the real risk isn't just in building the wealth. It's in keeping it.

This is where Modern Portfolio Theory, or MPT, enters the conversation. Now, before you tune out — assuming it's just another finance buzzword — let's strip it down to what really matters. MPT isn't about complicated math or academic debates. It's about one simple idea: you can't predict the future, but you can design a portfolio that's resilient enough to withstand it. At its heart, MPT says: don't bet your future on one horse, no matter how fast it's run so far. Bet on a carefully selected team, diversified enough that when — not if — surprises hit, you're still standing.

The brilliance of Modern Portfolio Theory is the concept of optimization — not maximizing returns at all costs, but maximizing return for a given level of risk. That word — risk — is where founders and traditional finance often part ways. As a founder, risk was your lifeblood. It's what you mastered. But building a company is different from managing post-liquidity wealth. In business, risk is strategic, calculated, often within your influence. In markets, risk is mostly blind and often indifferent to your effort or insight.

What MPT teaches is this: you can't eliminate risk, but you can design around it. By combining assets that don't move in lockstep — stocks, bonds, private equity, real estate, alternatives — you create a portfolio where the whole is stronger than any individual part. Some assets zig when others zag. Some surge when others slide. And while it feels counterintuitive, it's this blend — this sometimes messy, seemingly inefficient collection of uncorrelated assets — that produces the smoothest ride over time.

Now, founders often resist this idea at first. After all, it was betting on one big idea — their company — that got them here. Why diversify when conviction built the fortune? The answer lies in the difference between building wealth and preserving it. Concentration accelerates growth, but diversification preserves freedom. And at this stage of your life, freedom — to live, to give, to create without fear — is the real goal.

Let's bring it down to a real-world story. One founder I worked with had a massive position in his post-IPO stock, north of 80% of his liquid net worth. The company was a rocket ship. He hesitated to unwind — why diversify when returns were so strong? But we mapped it out: if the stock dropped by 50%, his entire lifestyle, his philanthropic plans, his family's financial security would all be compromised. Slowly, systematically, he built a diversified portfolio — public equities, private investments, some cash flow real estate, and high-quality municipal bonds. When the inevitable market correction hit two years later, his old stock fell hard — 60% off its peak. But his broader portfolio weathered the storm with only a modest decline, and most importantly, his goals stayed fully funded.

That's the quiet power of Modern Portfolio Theory. It's not exciting. It doesn't make headlines. It's slow, steady, resilient. But it's how you move from being rich on paper to being truly financially independent.

Of course, MPT isn't perfect. In times of severe crisis, correlations rise — meaning that assets that are supposed to move differently can all move down together. And traditional MPT models often assume that the future will look like the past. We know better. Markets evolve. Risks mutate. This is why modern wealth architecture doesn't stop at basic MPT — it layers in private investments, direct deals, alternatives, strategies uncorrelated to traditional markets. It customizes. It adjusts.

And that's where your advantage comes in. As a founder, you understand that no one-size-fits-all approach works. You don't need a cookie-cutter portfolio based on a template built for mass-affluent investors. You need a custom portfolio — one that reflects your specific liquidity needs, tax profile, legacy ambitions, and appetite for impact. MPT is the foundation, but the build-out — that's where real mastery happens.

So what's the action step here? It's time to move from theory to architecture. Look at your concentrated position and ask: if this were just one asset in a broader, optimized portfolio, what would the rest of the structure need to look like? How would I design around it — smoothing risk, ensuring liquidity, building resiliency? Who do I need on my team — tax advisors, investment architects, estate counsel — to build this right, not just fast?

Because the truth is, unwinding concentrated stock isn't just about reducing exposure. It's about reclaiming control. It's about shifting from reactive to proactive. From hoping the market holds up to ensuring your wealth holds up. From legacy built on luck to legacy built on purpose.

Modern Portfolio Theory, at its simplest, is about protecting what you've built without compromising who you are. It's about turning hard-won wealth into enduring freedom.

And freedom, after all, was the point of the whole journey, wasn't it?

Chapter 13: Risk Tolerance and Capacity: Know Thyself

You wouldn't have built what you built — scaled a company, weathered downturns, survived the chaos — without some serious risk appetite. It's in your DNA. Risk, for a founder or top executive, is not a four-letter word; it's a familiar, daily companion. But the relationship you once had with risk as a builder, a creator, is not the same relationship you should have with risk as a steward of concentrated wealth. Here's the quiet truth: the risk that built your wealth is not the same risk that will preserve it.

Too often, when I sit across from highly successful individuals like you, I find a dangerous mismatch — between risk tolerance and risk capacity. Risk tolerance is how much volatility you can sleep through at night. Risk capacity is how much volatility your financial situation can actually absorb without jeopardizing your goals. They're not the same. And when it comes to concentrated stock positions, failing to distinguish between the two can mean the difference between securing your legacy and unintentionally gambling it away.

Let's start with risk tolerance. This is emotional. It's personal. It's how you react when markets shake, when headlines scream, when the value of your concentrated stock swings by 30% or more. Some people thrive on it — they're wired to stomach the volatility. Others discover, only when the markets tremble, that they were less comfortable with risk than they thought. Knowing your true tolerance isn't about bravado. It's about honesty. It's about understanding that wealth is not a game — not anymore — and that peace of mind is a return on investment in itself.

Now, risk capacity. This is different. It's not emotional — it's mathematical. It's the hard analysis of how much you can afford to lose without derailing your life plans. If you have $100 million and only need $5 million to fund your ideal lifestyle, your capacity is enormous. If you have $20 million but future expenses and philanthropic goals that demand $15 million, your margin is thin. Risk capacity is what separates wealthy families that endure from those that don't.

And here's where it gets complicated: many founders and executives conflate the two. They think, "I can handle the ride," without asking, "Should I?" Your tolerance might be high — but if your capacity isn't, no amount of stomach for volatility will protect your family if things turn. Conversely, your capacity might be large, but your tolerance low — meaning you'll need a portfolio design that smooths volatility so you can stay the course. Mismatches are dangerous. They lead to panic selling at the wrong time or reckless risk-taking when restraint is needed most.

A real-world example: a tech founder I worked with had a staggering risk tolerance. He'd ridden his company through boom and bust cycles, layoffs, near-death moments. When his company went public, he held onto every share, convinced that volatility was just a badge of honor. But his post-IPO life wasn't built for the same swings. A 40% drop in his concentrated position suddenly threatened not just his lifestyle, but the endowment he planned to leave behind for medical research — a cause close to his heart. The problem wasn't that he couldn't stomach the loss. It was that his goals couldn't stomach the loss. We restructured. We unwound slowly, carefully, aligning his portfolio with both his emotional wiring and his financial needs.

When you're managing concentrated stock, understanding risk tolerance and capacity becomes even more critical. Concentration inherently means more volatility, more potential for sharp, damaging losses. Diversifying isn't just about maximizing returns — it's about engineering a portfolio that matches your real ability and willingness to take risk. It's about designing a strategy that lets you sleep at night, even when the markets don't.

So what's the action step? Start by separating the two. Don't guess. Assess. Work with a team that can help you model your financial capacity — your "need to risk" — against your emotional tolerance — your "willingness to risk." Build a strategy that honors both. If there's a gap, fix it. Better now than when volatility forces your hand.

And remember: true wealth is not just about enduring volatility — it's about navigating it wisely. Knowing your risk profile isn't a sign of weakness. It's a hallmark of stewardship. It's the move from being a founder to being a founder who endures — not just in business, but in family, in legacy, in life.

If you take nothing else from this chapter, take this: the goal isn't to avoid risk. It's to understand it. To respect it. To align it with your future, not your past. Because wealth, once built, is no longer about conquest. It's about careful, intentional protection. It's about freedom — and freedom, after all, isn't measured in dollars, but in the ability to live without fear.

Chapter 14: Time Horizon, Matching Money to Purpose

When you built your company, you had a clear sense of time. Not just the day-to-day sprints, but the longer arcs — product roadmaps, market entry timelines, funding milestones. You understood intuitively that success wasn't a sprint; it was a series of strategic, deliberate moves paced over years. Managing concentrated wealth is no different. In fact, the single most important — and most overlooked — discipline when unwinding concentrated stock is matching money to purpose through the lens of time horizon.

Too often, highly successful founders and executives assume that wealth is static — a pile of assets to be managed. But wealth is not static. It's dynamic, and your financial needs and goals move across time. If you don't align your wealth with these moving targets, you risk mismatches that could either imperil your lifestyle or squander your opportunities. The real work isn't just about deciding when to sell stock — it's about knowing what you'll need and when you'll need it.

Let's break this down simply. Money for short-term needs — liquidity for lifestyle spending, for tax payments, for philanthropy you want to engage in over the next few years — needs to be safe, stable, predictable. It can't be at the mercy of market volatility or an illiquid, undiversified position. The time horizon for these dollars is short. The purpose is immediate. Risk, here, is your enemy.

Contrast that with money earmarked for longer-term goals — endowing a foundation, funding multi-generational trusts, or creating legacy investments in impact-driven ventures. This money doesn't need to perform this year or even this decade. It needs to grow intelligently, aligned with timelines that stretch decades beyond your lifetime. Here, the time horizon invites a different kind of thinking. Volatility in the short term may be acceptable — even desirable — if it comes with the reward of long-term growth.

Real-world example: A founder I advised post-IPO had just cleared a nine-figure liquidity event. He wanted to buy a primary residence, fund a donor-advised fund for philanthropy, and start an investment pool for his children's future — all at once. The mistake would have been treating these different goals with the same investment strategy. Instead, we allocated capital into different "buckets," each matched to the intended time horizon. Immediate needs were placed in ultra-safe, highly liquid vehicles. Intermediate goals were assigned moderate risk with a five- to seven-year horizon. Long-term legacy funds were invested with a 20-plus-year view, accepting more equity exposure. The result: clarity, security, and optimized growth — without unnecessary risk.

Here's the nuance: concentrated stock almost never fits neatly into a time horizon framework. It's liquid if public, yes, but it's volatile and tax-sensitive. It's illiquid if private, and often impossible to time perfectly. This is why concentrated stock shouldn't be your liquidity plan. It should be a source of potential long-term value — a resource to be managed methodically, not a piggy bank to be broken reactively.

So how do you proceed? Start by mapping your future obligations and aspirations across timelines — what money you'll need in one year, in five years, in 20 years. Then, design your asset allocation around those timelines, using diversification to de-risk your short-term and mid-term needs, while thoughtfully allocating long-term capital for growth. Unwinding concentrated stock is a critical part of this — because without diversified, purpose-matched assets, your time horizon becomes hostage to the whims of a single company's fortunes.

Another client — a brilliant early employee in a now-famous tech giant — refused to sell his shares even after becoming liquid. He thought, "Why sell a winner?" But when he wanted to fund his daughter's college education and found himself forced to sell shares after a 30% drop, the pain was real. He hadn't matched his money to his purpose. He'd matched it to a hope. Hope is not a strategy. Time horizon alignment is.

There's an emotional shift that happens when you match money to purpose across time. Anxiety drops. Clarity rises. You stop seeing wealth as a volatile scoreboard and start seeing it as a structured, intentional architecture designed to support your best life. The short term becomes secure. The long term becomes powerful. And you regain control.

So here's your invitation: sit down with your advisory team and map your time horizons. Get precise. Understand not just what you own, but when you'll need it — and for what. Build investment strategies that honor that calendar. Don't let the tail — your concentrated position — wag the dog — your life's purpose and legacy.

Because in the end, concentrated wealth isn't just about protecting assets. It's about protecting the life — and the impact — those assets were meant to create. Time horizon discipline isn't a luxury. It's your new financial foundation.

Take one step today: sketch your timeline. Write down what you'll need in the next one, five, and 20 years. If you can't match your assets to that plan today, it's time to rethink the plan. Freedom, after all, isn't having assets. It's having assets you can rely on — when you need them — without fear.

Chapter 15: The Power of Rebalancing, Automated Discipline

If there's one thing that separates professional investors from everyone else, it's not intelligence. It's discipline. Disciplined decision-making wins over brilliant guesswork, year after year. And at the ultra-high-net-worth level, where the stakes are high and the room for error is narrow, discipline isn't a nice-to-have. It's non-negotiable. One of the simplest, yet most powerful, tools to build that discipline into your wealth strategy is rebalancing.

Let's be honest: when you've spent a career building, scaling, and perhaps exiting a successful company, the last thing you want is to lose the fruits of that labor to complacency. And yet, the story of many concentrated stock holders is a cautionary one — they let inertia guide their wealth. Rebalancing is the antidote to inertia. It's the quiet, systematic practice of periodically reviewing your asset allocation and adjusting it back to its original design. It sounds simple. It is simple. But its power is profound.

Imagine this: you have an initial allocation — say 60% diversified equities, 30% bonds, 10% alternatives. Over time, if equities rally and bonds lag, your portfolio drifts. You might find yourself sitting at 75% equities, 20% bonds, 5% alternatives without ever making a conscious choice. Your risk profile has shifted silently — and dangerously. Left unchecked, this drift can magnify your exposure, making you vulnerable to downturns just when you think you're coasting.

Now, layer in a concentrated stock position. Maybe it starts at 30% of your net worth. But as your company grows — or the market inflates your stock — that 30% balloons to 50% or 60%. Suddenly, your financial well-being is tethered to one name, one sector, one business cycle. Without regular rebalancing, concentration risk creeps in silently until it's the dominant force in your portfolio.

One founder I worked with learned this the hard way. He had diversified his IPO windfall initially, but over the next decade, as his former company's stock continued to outperform, he resisted selling more. By the time he realized the imbalance, his family's future was almost entirely dependent on one public stock. When a downturn hit, he watched not just his net worth decline, but his peace of mind evaporate.

Rebalancing is not about predicting markets. It's about restoring alignment. It's an act of humility — a reminder that markets move, valuations change, and no single asset should outweigh your broader objectives. It forces you to sell high and buy low systematically — harvesting gains from overperforming assets and reinvesting in underperformers. Over decades, this simple act compounds not just returns, but stability.

For holders of concentrated stock, rebalancing can feel emotionally painful. Selling shares of a company you founded or helped build can feel like betrayal. But this isn't about rejecting your past success. It's about protecting your future freedom. Automated rebalancing removes the emotion. Set the guardrails. Program the adjustments. Step back and let discipline do its work.

There's also a tax conversation here. Intelligent rebalancing isn't blind. It's tax-aware. It seeks to minimize taxable events by leveraging tax-loss harvesting, charitable gifting, or gradually diversifying through structured sales strategies. It's a conversation about efficiency as much as it is about discipline — how to preserve gains while methodically unwinding risks.

Another client I advised implemented a rebalancing strategy using a donor-advised fund. Every year, he would gift appreciated shares of his company stock to his DAF, reducing his taxable estate, securing a charitable deduction, and gradually unwinding his concentration. At the same time, he rebalanced the proceeds into a diversified pool of investments aligned with his family's long-term goals. Slow. Systematic. Effective.

The key takeaway? Rebalancing is not a one-time event. It's a discipline. It's the quiet, automated cadence that keeps your wealth strategy honest. It's the unseen hand that protects you from the emotional traps of overconfidence and inertia. And at this stage of your life, discipline — not bravado — is what builds dynasties.

So here's your call to action: audit your portfolio today. How often do you rebalance? Is it automated, or is it emotional? Does your plan address the growing influence of your concentrated position? If not, it's time to layer in the discipline you deserve. Time to treat your wealth with the same rigor you once treated your business.

Because wealth without discipline is fragile. But wealth governed by disciplined, intentional action — that's the foundation of true, lasting freedom. Don't leave it to chance. Build the system now — and let it protect you when you need it most.

Chapter 16: Cash Flow and Liquidity Planning for Entrepreneurs

Let's start with a truth that isn't often discussed at this level: wealth is not the same as cash flow. You can be rich on paper and still be poor when it comes to liquidity. For entrepreneurs and founders who have built and scaled companies, this distinction becomes stark after an exit or a major liquidity event. Your balance sheet may glow with impressive numbers, but unless you've designed a deliberate cash flow and liquidity strategy, you can quickly find yourself asset-rich and cash-poor.

In the world you've lived in — building businesses, raising capital, navigating growth cycles — cash flow was king. Your operating business had its ebbs and flows, but the mission was always clear: manage working capital, fuel growth, sustain operations. Personal cash flow planning, however, is a different game. It's not about scaling — it's about sustaining. It's about converting concentrated, often illiquid, wealth into a life strategy that ensures stability, optionality, and peace of mind.

The mistake many successful founders make is assuming the liquidity event itself solves the liquidity problem. They sell a company or exercise stock options, triggering a windfall, and believe the hard part is over. In reality, the hard part is just beginning. Without a structured liquidity plan, taxes erode more than necessary, investment portfolios are assembled haphazardly, and large capital purchases — homes, planes, investments in friends' startups — drain resources faster than expected.

Take a founder I recently advised: post-exit, he had $100 million in equity, most of it locked up in restricted stock units and long lock-up agreements. His net worth had exploded, but his available cash? Slim. Personal expenses continued — lifestyle, philanthropy, new ventures — but the liquidity to support them lagged behind. He found himself forced to fire-sale assets and borrow against his stock holdings in unfavorable markets. Not because he wasn't wealthy. But because he wasn't liquid.

Liquidity is the buffer between wealth and freedom. It's what ensures that you don't have to sell at the wrong time, under the wrong conditions. It gives you negotiating power, patience, and peace. The right liquidity plan begins by asking a simple, powerful question: how much of your balance sheet is genuinely available for use in the next 12 to 36 months, without severe tax or market penalties?

The other side of liquidity is cash flow. Many founders underestimate what their new life costs. Not because they're extravagant, but because the structure changes. Taxes on stock sales. Capital calls from private equity funds. Charitable commitments. Family support structures. Legacy expenses like foundation funding and next-generation education costs. These aren't one-off expenses — they're part of a broader cash flow story that needs proactive planning.

A comprehensive liquidity and cash flow strategy should include a few core elements: a personal operating account, like a working capital account for your life; a reserve fund to cover 12 to 24 months of expenses, sitting somewhere accessible and relatively safe; a thoughtful debt structure, if any, tied to long-term assets rather than lifestyle spending; and an investment portfolio calibrated not just for returns, but for tax efficiency and risk mitigation.

Another client handled this masterfully. He set aside five years' worth of lifestyle spending in a laddered municipal bond portfolio, giving him tax-advantaged income and liquidity without needing to tap into equity markets during downturns. He structured a donor-advised fund to manage his charitable giving, front-loading contributions in high-income years. And he built a cash flow model — not a static one, but one that accounted for dynamic life changes like future business ventures and family events.

Planning like this isn't glamorous. It doesn't make headlines. But it builds resilience. It ensures that when opportunities arise, you're not scrambling for liquidity. And when volatility hits — because it always does — you're not forced to liquidate assets at inopportune moments. Liquidity planning turns wealth into freedom, not just a number on a statement.

And let's not ignore the psychological benefit. Knowing your cash flow is secured, knowing liquidity buffers are in place — it changes how you operate. It restores the entrepreneurial freedom you had when you first built your company: the freedom to say no, the freedom to wait, the freedom to dream bigger without fear.

So here's the question: if you had no income for the next three years, would your lifestyle — your impact, your ambitions — be secure without selling assets at a loss? If the answer isn't a confident yes, it's time to design a liquidity and cash flow plan that matches the ambition of the life you've built.

Because unwinding a concentrated stock position isn't just about reducing risk. It's about liberating yourself from dependence on a single asset. It's about building a structure that empowers your choices — not one that limits them.

The call to action? Schedule a personal liquidity review. Audit not just your assets, but your accessible assets. Build a cash flow model that matches your new reality — and plan for the life you want, not the one you're reacting to.

At this level, wealth without liquidity is a liability. But wealth with a deliberate, disciplined liquidity strategy? That's power. That's stewardship. That's freedom — real freedom.

Chapter 17: Tax-Loss Harvesting, What It Is and Why It's Gold

When you've spent your life building, scaling, and leading, the idea that losing could somehow be winning feels counterintuitive. After all, you didn't reach this point in your career by celebrating losses. But in wealth strategy — real wealth strategy — there's an art to using loss as leverage. And nowhere is that more evident than in tax-loss harvesting.

Let's begin with the simple but powerful concept: tax-loss harvesting is the process of selling securities at a loss to offset capital gains elsewhere in your portfolio. It turns unrealized losses into tangible tax savings, reducing your bill to Uncle Sam while keeping your investment strategy intact. Done correctly, it's not just smart — it's gold.

Consider a scenario you may know well: you've accumulated a concentrated position in your company's stock over decades. Meanwhile, you've diversified around the edges, but some of your satellite investments — maybe a venture fund position, maybe a small-cap tech ETF — have underperformed. In an ordinary world, you might let those losses sit, hesitant to sell for less than you paid. In the world of sophisticated wealth management, you recognize the opportunity to harvest those losses, apply them against the gains from your concentrated stock, and dramatically cut your net tax exposure.

The beauty of tax-loss harvesting is that it doesn't have to disrupt your investment philosophy. Say you sell a lagging technology ETF at a loss. IRS rules prevent you from repurchasing the exact same security for 30 days — known as the wash-sale rule — but nothing stops you from reinvesting in a similar, not substantially identical fund. Your market exposure remains, but your tax bill shrinks. You've protected your strategy while optimizing your tax footprint.

The power compounds over time. Unused harvested losses can be carried forward indefinitely. If you offset $500,000 in gains this year but only realize $300,000 in losses, the remaining $200,000 carries forward into the future — ammunition against next year's gains or even the gains that come a decade from now. In other words, harvesting is not a one-time maneuver. It's a discipline, a long-term strategy that adds silent but significant value to your overall financial architecture.

Yet many ultra-affluent individuals neglect this tool. Why? Sometimes it's emotional — an aversion to selling at a loss, a reluctance to admit a decision didn't pan out as hoped. Sometimes it's logistical — portfolios that aren't actively managed or advisors who don't have the bandwidth to monitor positions daily. And sometimes it's psychological — the false belief that large fortunes are impervious to incremental gains. But the reality is this: at your level, marginal gains are millions. A 1% tax improvement across a $50 million portfolio isn't academic — it's real money, real freedom.

Take a real-world case I encountered: a founder who had sold a significant portion of their company stock after an IPO, triggering a multi-million-dollar gain. At the same time, the broader market experienced a downturn, and their passive index investments were temporarily underwater. Through disciplined tax-loss harvesting, we offset over $4 million in realized gains, slashing the founder's tax bill by seven figures. The portfolio recovered over time — as they always planned it would — but the tax savings were locked in immediately.

Another founder — equally successful — resisted harvesting losses, preferring to "wait it out" and avoid "locking in failure." When he eventually needed liquidity and sold at a less opportune time, he faced not only a larger tax bill but fewer offsetting losses to cushion the impact. Pride cost him dearly — not in public reputation, but in silent erosion of wealth.

The lesson is clear: tax-loss harvesting isn't about admitting defeat. It's about strategic surrender in service of a larger victory. It's about recognizing that wealth mastery isn't just about what you earn — it's about what you keep. And keeping more, while staying fully invested and aligned with your strategy, is the hallmark of sophisticated financial stewardship.

If you haven't yet incorporated a disciplined tax-loss harvesting strategy into your wealth plan, the time is now. Start with a simple question: when was the last time someone scanned your portfolio for strategic loss opportunities? If the answer isn't "recently and routinely," there's an immediate opportunity to improve.

Because unwinding concentrated stock positions isn't just about selling shares — it's about building the structures around those sales to optimize every dollar, every gain, and yes, even every loss. It's about turning what looks like weakness into a source of lasting strength.

Take this as your invitation to review your approach. Schedule a full portfolio audit with a tax-savvy advisor. Commit to a harvesting calendar — not ad hoc, but methodical. Make tax-loss harvesting a pillar of your wealth management strategy, not an afterthought.

At this level, there are no small wins. There are only smart wins. And tax-loss harvesting? It's one of the smartest — and quietest — tools at your disposal.

Chapter 18: Understanding Cost Basis and Capital Gains

One of the sharpest tools in your wealth management toolkit — and frankly, one of the most misunderstood — is the concept of cost basis. It's a seemingly simple number, but for someone in your position, it can quietly determine how much of your hard-earned wealth you get to keep and how much you hand over to the IRS. When you hold significant concentrated stock, understanding your cost basis isn't just academic; it's strategic.

Let's ground this in the basics. Your cost basis is, essentially, what you paid for your shares — adjusted over time for things like stock splits, dividends reinvested, or additional purchases. It's the foundation against which any future gains are measured. The spread between your cost basis and your sale price is what creates a capital gain — and it's that gain, not the full sale price, that's taxed.

At first glance, this sounds straightforward. You buy at $5, sell at $50, you've made $45 per share, and the IRS wants its piece. But for founders, early employees, or executives with concentrated stock, the reality is much more nuanced. Your shares likely have different acquisition dates and prices. Some may be from early purchases, some from options exercises, some from RSUs that vested over time. Each block — each "lot," in tax parlance — can have a different cost basis.

Why does this matter? Because when you begin unwinding, when you start selling down your position, you have choices. You can specify which shares to sell — high-basis or low-basis. Selling higher-basis shares first can minimize your immediate tax liability. Selling low-basis shares may lock in larger gains — but could make sense if you anticipate higher tax rates in the future or want to "clean up" the position now while markets are favorable. These are not small decisions. They can shift millions in taxable income from one year to another.

Now, let's layer on another complexity: capital gains tax rates. In the U.S., if you hold an asset for more than a year before selling, you generally qualify for long-term capital gains treatment — a much more favorable rate than short-term gains. Short-term gains are taxed at ordinary income rates, which can climb as high as 37% federally (plus state taxes). Long-term gains, by contrast, are typically taxed at 15% or 20%, depending on your income bracket. That difference is not theoretical. On an eight-figure exit, it's real dollars, real freedom.

I worked with a founder who had accumulated a large block of pre-IPO shares with a near-zero basis. Post-IPO, the temptation was to sell immediately — understandably so, given the massive paper gains. But moving too quickly would have triggered short-term gains. By developing a plan to hold for the long-term mark — strategically selling only after the one-year threshold — we reduced the client's effective tax rate by nearly 20%, translating to tens of millions saved.

Contrast that with another executive who, feeling the heat of volatility, rushed into selling large portions of their concentrated stock within months of their company's IPO. The ordinary income tax bill was staggering, compounded by state taxes in a high-tax jurisdiction. Had they waited just a few months longer, the difference could have funded a legacy project, endowed a foundation, or simply offered more financial flexibility for decades.

Another often-overlooked element is the role of charitable giving. Donating low-basis shares to a donor-advised fund or a private foundation can eliminate capital gains tax on the appreciation — and allow you to claim a charitable deduction at the full fair market value. It's a strategy that serves dual purposes: reducing concentrated risk while maximizing philanthropic impact and minimizing tax exposure. In a world where you're already thinking bigger — legacy, impact, stewardship — this becomes an elegant move, not a sacrifice.

Of course, managing cost basis is not just about avoiding tax today. It's about optimizing over your entire wealth horizon. Sometimes, realizing a gain now — even at a high tax rate — makes sense if the investment outlook is deteriorating or if diversification priorities outweigh tax minimization. Other times, it's about staggering sales to avoid stacking gains into a single year and pushing yourself into punitive tax brackets or net investment income taxes.

Sophisticated wealth planning at your level requires not just understanding your cost basis, but actively managing it — integrating it into your larger liquidity plan, your estate plan, and your philanthropic vision. It's about knowing not just what you own, but how you own it, when to sell it, and what that sale means across your balance sheet and your broader life goals.

If you haven't had a recent conversation about your cost basis — if you couldn't tell me within five minutes your basis profile across your concentrated stock holdings — then this is the time to pause. To reflect. To act.

Schedule a detailed cost basis audit. Not a cursory review, but a granular, lot-by-lot analysis. Work with your advisor and CPA to simulate different unwind scenarios — what happens if you sell this year versus next? High-basis first or low-basis? Harvesting charitable deductions or gifting appreciated shares? Model it all, because these decisions are too significant to leave to instinct or habit.

The ultimate goal isn't just to lower this year's tax bill. It's to create clarity, control, and flexibility. To give yourself more tools, not fewer. More freedom, not less. To steward not just the numbers on a spreadsheet, but the life and legacy those numbers are meant to enable.

Because unwinding concentrated stock is never just about diversifying assets — it's about concentrating your focus on what matters most: freedom, control, and stewardship. And it starts with mastering one of the simplest, yet most powerful concepts in your arsenal — your cost basis.

Chapter 19: Short-Term vs. Long-Term Gains, Timing Your Moves

There's a moment every founder, executive, or early employee with concentrated stock will face. It usually comes after the IPO lockup period ends or following a significant corporate event. You sit down, you open your portfolio, and you realize: the numbers on that screen are no longer hypothetical. They're real — and so are the decisions you now have to make. One of the most critical? Understanding the difference between short-term and long-term capital gains, and the massive implications of when — not just how — you choose to sell.

Let's start with what's at stake. In the U.S. tax code, not all gains are treated equally. Sell stock you've held for less than a year, and you'll pay taxes on the gain at your ordinary income rate — which for high earners can run up to 37% federally, not including state taxes. Sell after you've held for a year and a day? You drop into the much more favorable long-term capital gains bracket — generally 15% or 20%, depending on your income level. That differential might not feel dramatic when you're talking about small numbers. But when your gain is in the tens, or hundreds, of millions? The difference can be staggering.

I once sat with a founder who was eager to diversify immediately after their company's IPO. The stock was volatile, they felt exposed, and the temptation to sell right away was palpable. But rushing would have meant paying north of 40% in combined federal and state taxes. By patiently working with a staged sales plan — and carefully crossing the one-year threshold — they dropped their effective tax rate by over 15 percentage points. That shift alone freed up millions of dollars for further investment, philanthropy, and personal liquidity.

Of course, tax isn't the only variable here. Risk management matters too. Sometimes, holding out for long-term status exposes you to market volatility you may not be comfortable with. If the stock falls dramatically during that waiting period, the potential tax savings could be wiped out by unrealized losses. Timing isn't just about tax brackets; it's about balance — weighing tax efficiency against market risk and personal liquidity needs.

Then there's the behavioral side. Founders and early employees often have an emotional tie to their stock. You know the company inside and out. You've lived through the 2 a.m. product launches, the pivots, the board meetings, the blood and sweat. That familiarity can breed a dangerous bias — an overconfidence that your stock will keep rising, that waiting longer always pays off. Sometimes it does. Sometimes it doesn't. The key is not to let emotion hijack rational planning.

Another layer to consider: charitable giving. Holding appreciated stock for over a year before donating it can allow you to claim a charitable deduction for the full fair market value — and completely avoid paying capital gains tax on the appreciation. That's an elegant tax strategy, but it only works if you satisfy the long-term holding requirement. If philanthropy is part of your broader wealth and legacy plan — and for many ultra-high-net-worth individuals, it is — the timing of your sale or donation becomes even more critical.

Liquidity strategy also intersects with timing. Let's say you're planning a major real estate purchase, a private investment, or even establishing a family office. Knowing when liquidity will be available — and at what cost — can influence whether you're willing to accept short-term tax penalties for the sake of immediacy, or whether it's better to wait, unlock the long-term rate, and move forward with greater financial efficiency.

Some founders employ hedging strategies — collars, prepaid variable forwards, or structured sales — to manage risk while they wait out the one-year clock. These tools aren't free, and they introduce complexity, but they can offer a way to balance risk reduction with tax optimization. Structuring these correctly is an art, not just a science, and it requires advisors who understand both the nuance of your stock's volatility and your broader financial plan.

Real-world mistakes are instructive too. I recall a highly compensated early employee who deferred selling for emotional reasons — "just a little longer," he kept saying. The market turned. His company's stock, once a market darling, tumbled 60%. By the time he hit the one-year mark, his net proceeds, even at the lower tax rate, were dramatically less than if he had sold earlier, accepted the higher tax rate, and locked in his gains. In wealth management, perfect tax strategy without risk awareness is no strategy at all.

The real goal is to move from reactive decision-making to proactive planning. Set parameters ahead of time: What's your drop-dead date for triggering a sale, regardless of tax status? How much downside are you willing to tolerate in pursuit of lower tax rates? How does this decision fit into your broader liquidity, legacy, and investment strategy? Timing your moves is not about gambling on the calendar — it's about aligning your actions with your highest priorities and tolerances.

If you're holding a substantial concentrated stock position, now is the time to map it out. Build a plan that factors in your acquisition dates, current market conditions, future liquidity needs, and personal tax situation. Don't leave timing to chance or emotion. Precision in timing can be the quiet difference between a good outcome and a truly transformational one.

Ultimately, unwinding concentrated stock isn't about avoiding taxes altogether — it's about minimizing unnecessary friction, maximizing strategic flexibility, and, most of all, protecting and growing the freedom your success has earned. And that process starts with a simple but profound truth: not all gains are created equal. Timing matters — more than you might think.

Chapter 20: How Financial Literacy Empowers Better Decisions

There's a common misconception among highly successful individuals: the idea that being exceptional at building a business automatically translates into being exceptional at managing wealth. The truth is, they are completely different skill sets. One is about risk, innovation, leadership, and relentless execution. The other is about stewardship, preservation, tax strategy, and understanding the invisible hand that guides capital markets. Sitting across from founders, executives, and early employees with concentrated stock, I often see the same realization unfold — that what got them here won't necessarily get them where they want to go next.

Financial literacy, at its core, is not about memorizing terms or mastering esoteric investment theories. It's about understanding how to ask better questions. It's about seeing through complexity, recognizing when you're being sold to versus advised, and knowing how different pieces of your wealth ecosystem interact — taxes with investments, liquidity with risk, legacy planning with asset allocation. And when you hold a concentrated stock position, those intersections aren't just technical details. They are the difference between financial freedom and financial fragility.

Take, for example, the decision of when — and how — to begin unwinding your stock. Without a clear grasp of how cost basis affects capital gains, how short-term versus long-term taxation plays out, or how selling strategies can integrate with charitable vehicles like donor-advised funds or CRUTs

(Charitable Remainder Unitrusts), even a "successful" sale can leave millions unnecessarily lost to taxes. I once worked with a founder who had an eight-figure paper gain, but hadn't considered tax-loss harvesting opportunities from prior years that could have shielded part of the gain. Basic literacy around carryforward losses turned what could have been a large tax bill into a far smaller, much more strategic one.

Financial literacy also empowers better judgment in choosing advisors. Too often, ultra-high-net-worth individuals are prey to advisors who dazzle with jargon but deliver little strategy. When you're literate, you can filter signal from noise. You can differentiate between those offering cookie-cutter solutions and those crafting strategies tailored to your specific situation — your liquidity timelines, your philanthropic goals, your family governance structures. You move from being a passive client to an active CEO of your financial life.

And let's talk about risk — because real literacy reveals the risks you don't see. Holding concentrated stock isn't just a portfolio issue; it's a lifestyle risk, a legacy risk, a risk to optionality. Literacy sharpens your ability to spot concentration risk not as a theoretical probability, but as a real threat to the autonomy you've spent a lifetime building. It shifts the conversation from, "What's the stock price today?" to, "How exposed am I to single-asset volatility, and what's my Plan B?"

I've seen firsthand how literate founders make better liquidity plans. One founder I advised had a significant position in a rapidly growing tech company. Rather than viewing their wealth as an amorphous lump tied to a single stock, they built a detailed liquidity ladder — understanding their lockup schedules, modeling different sale scenarios, stress-testing market conditions, and layering in structured sale strategies to gradually diversify over several years. They didn't move impulsively. They moved intelligently — and they protected their upside without risking their foundation.

Another founder, equally brilliant but less literate, waited too long. They understood their product, their company, and their market better than anyone. But they didn't understand how interest rate environments impacted the value of deferred compensation. They didn't appreciate how quickly concentrated stock can lose its market halo in a downturn. By the time they decided to act, the window had narrowed, and what could have been a disciplined, strategic unwind became a rushed, reactive liquidation — with far less advantageous terms.

Financial literacy also reframes how you think about legacy. If you understand how different trusts operate, how philanthropic vehicles can be leveraged, how family governance structures can be embedded into your financial planning, you start building not just for yourself but for generations. You shift from optimizing net worth to optimizing generational impact. You ensure that your wealth becomes a platform — not a prison — for your heirs.

The most important thing literacy gives you, however, is agency. It removes the fear that can paralyze even the most successful individuals when it comes to their wealth. It replaces confusion with confidence. It replaces anxiety with action. It gives you the language and the logic to engage meaningfully with your advisory team, to chart a course that reflects your priorities — not someone else's model portfolio.

So, what does better decision-making look like in practice? It looks like setting a planned liquidity calendar years in advance. It looks like pre-determining trigger points for selling based on tax strategy and market conditions, not emotions. It looks like educating the next generation early, involving them in philanthropic discussions, preparing them not just to inherit wealth but to steward it. It looks like building a financial operating system that's as intentional as the business you built from scratch.

Let me leave you with this: unwinding concentrated stock is not a transaction. It's a transition — from wealth builder to wealth steward. Financial literacy is the bridge that makes that transition successful. The question isn't whether you're smart enough. You are. The question is whether you're equipped with the right lens to make the next right move.

The first step is simple but powerful: audit your current financial knowledge. Identify one area where you feel unsure — taxes, liquidity planning, asset allocation, charitable strategy — and make it a priority to deepen your understanding. Bring in experts, yes. But bring yourself to the table first — armed with knowledge, clarity, and intent. Because the greatest risk is not what happens in the market. It's what happens when you stop learning.

Synopsis: Part III — Tools of the Trade: Strategies for Unwinding Concentration

By the time you arrive at this stage, you've grasped the critical importance of diversifying concentrated wealth. Now it's time to shift from understanding *why* to mastering *how*. Part III is your strategic playbook — a deep dive into the sophisticated financial tools and techniques designed to help you unwind concentrated stock positions with precision, tax efficiency, and purpose.

This section is not about theory. It's about application. We walk through proven strategies used by founders, executives, and high-net-worth individuals to systematically de-risk, unlock liquidity, and preserve upside. From selling disciplines like 10b5-1 plans to advanced solutions like exchange funds, collars, prepaid variable forwards, and charitable remainder trusts (CRTs), you'll see the mechanics and mindset required to navigate the transition intelligently.

But we don't just present a menu of options — we show you how to match each strategy to your unique goals, tax profile, and time horizon. You'll understand the trade-offs: liquidity versus control, flexibility versus commitment, simplicity versus sophistication. Real-world examples bring these strategies to life, revealing the costs of inaction and the rewards of intentionality.

This part of the book reinforces a central truth: unwinding a concentrated position is not about abandoning your past success. It's about protecting it. It's about converting illiquid potential into diversified resilience — freeing your capital to serve a broader mission: your life, your family, your legacy.

Part III empowers you to move from indecision to action, from risk to resilience, from concentrated wealth to enduring financial freedom. This is where your next chapter — the chapter after the liquidity event — truly begins.

Chapter 21: 10b5-1 Plans, Pre-Arranged Sales Without Insider Risk

When you hold a significant position in a company—whether as a founder, executive, or early employee—selling your stock isn't just a financial transaction. It's a legal minefield. You're not just moving money; you're stepping into a world governed by SEC regulations, insider trading restrictions, and market optics. And if you're not careful, even a perfectly innocent sale can raise eyebrows or trigger investigations. This is where 10b5-1 plans come into play—a tool designed not just to create liquidity, but to protect you from allegations of insider trading and to allow you to navigate concentration risk strategically, not emotionally.

Imagine this: you've just wrapped up a quarterly earnings call. You're sitting on a huge position—tens of millions of dollars in unrealized gains—but you know that if you sell now, while you're privy to non-public information, you could be exposed to insider trading accusations. So you wait. And the market moves against you. The window you thought you had closes. This cycle repeats quarter after quarter. Your personal liquidity remains hostage to the company's disclosure calendar. That's the trap that founders and executives fall into. 10b5-1 plans are your way out.

A 10b5-1 plan is a pre-arranged, SEC-sanctioned trading plan. It allows insiders like you to sell stock on a predetermined schedule, according to rules you set up at a time when you are not in possession of material nonpublic information (MNPI). Once the plan is in place, it operates automatically—immune to whatever inside knowledge you later acquire. This structure creates a protective legal shield, ensuring your sales are seen as above-board, pre-planned, and non-reactive.

Setting up a 10b5-1 plan requires strategy, not just form-filling. The plan must define the amount, price, and date (or a formula for determining those parameters) for future sales. It's critical that the plan reflects a disciplined, rational unwinding of your concentrated position. No games. No backdoors. And because these plans are public disclosures in many cases, they send a message to the market about your professionalism and governance standards. Done right, they are not just a legal shield—they are a credibility asset.

But let's be clear: 10b5-1 plans aren't perfect. They require careful calibration. You can't tweak or cancel a plan mid-flight without raising suspicion or, in some cases, invalidating the protections. Once the plan is in motion, you're committed. And while the SEC recently updated rules around 10b5-1 plans—including cooling-off periods and limitations on overlapping plans—the fundamental principle remains: discipline and predictability trump emotional, reactive decision-making.

Consider a founder who failed to set up a plan, relying instead on opportunistic, discretionary sales. After a strong earnings report, they sold a chunk of shares—unaware that the SEC was closely monitoring patterns. Though no misconduct was found, the optics damaged both reputation and valuation. Now contrast that with an executive who set up a 10b5-1 plan immediately post-IPO, gradually and invisibly diversifying over a two-year horizon. The difference wasn't just legal protection—it was peace of mind, a smoother market reception, and a personal financial plan that wasn't held hostage by the company's news cycles.

There are nuances to consider. For example, plan timing relative to company events (M&A talks, new product launches), diversification strategies within the sales schedule (selling more gradually to minimize market impact), and tax considerations around long-term capital gains. Crafting a 10b5-1 plan isn't about filling in a template. It's about precision, architecture, and alignment with your broader financial goals.

One key advantage is the emotional relief a 10b5-1 plan provides. It removes the psychological burden of timing the market. No more second-guessing yourself. No more stress over news releases, stock dips, or trading windows. Instead, you shift from reactive decision-making to strategic execution. Your wealth strategy moves from hope to systematization.

If you're sitting on a concentrated stock position, understand this: a 10b5-1 plan isn't about surrendering control—it's about redefining it. It's about taking the volatility of public perception and regulatory scrutiny out of your personal liquidity equation. It's about protecting what you've built, both in terms of financial capital and reputational capital.

Here's the simple truth: the most successful founders, executives, and early employees I've worked with don't leave liquidity up to chance. They don't let windows dictate their lives. They architect liquidity with intention. They deploy strategies like 10b5-1 plans not because they're nervous, but because they're smart—and they know that freedom, clarity, and legacy are built not on hope, but on structure.

You didn't build your wealth randomly. Don't leave its preservation to randomness either. A 10b5-1 plan is more than a regulatory necessity—it's a tool for freedom. It's a way to control risk, secure liquidity, and maintain your integrity in a world where perception matters. If you haven't built one yet, or if yours hasn't been reviewed in light of recent SEC updates, it's time. Consult your team—your wealth advisor, your legal counsel—and design the structure that will give you the confidence to move forward deliberately.

Because in this game, discipline isn't optional. It's everything.

Chapter 22: Selling Gradually, How to Exit Over Time

There's a powerful temptation, when you hold a large, concentrated stock position, to think in binaries: either hold forever or sell everything at once. But when you sit where you are now—ultra-affluent, sophisticated, aware that your single-stock exposure is both a blessing and a burden—the smart path isn't either extreme. It's methodical. It's measured. It's gradual.

Let's start with a familiar feeling. You've built or helped build something extraordinary. Your concentrated stock position is more than just a financial asset—it's a monument to years of work, sacrifice, and risk-taking. But therein lies the trap: emotional attachment clouds rational judgment. If the stock falls, regret can be overwhelming. If it rises, selling feels like betrayal or bad timing. Paralysis sets in. And yet, doing nothing is itself a decision—a risky one.

The key is to move from reactive thinking to strategic action. Selling gradually—executing a disciplined, phased unwinding of your concentrated position—offers a path that balances the need for liquidity, the desire for upside, and the demand for tax efficiency. It's not about market timing; it's about market strategy.

One of the biggest benefits of selling gradually is risk mitigation. Markets move unpredictably. A single earnings miss, a regulatory surprise, or a shift in investor sentiment can take your concentrated position down 20%, 30%, or more—overnight. Selling over time hedges you against bad timing. You don't have to predict the peak. You just have to capture a good average.

Consider how a founder I worked with approached this. She held a concentrated position worth $90 million at the IPO. She believed fervently in the company's future. But she also understood that belief isn't a substitute for strategy. Instead of dumping shares into the market, she set up a staged selling plan—pre-arranged sales over three years, increasing liquidity without alarming the market or herself. She captured gains, reduced risk, and preserved her psychological comfort. She wasn't chasing tops or running from dips. She was executing a plan.

Gradual selling also has tax advantages. By selling over time, you can harvest long-term capital gains rather than incurring higher short-term rates. You can manage your income recognition year by year, staying in lower tax brackets or using charitable strategies like Donor-Advised Funds to offset taxable gains. You gain the flexibility to react to changing tax laws, market conditions, and your personal financial needs.

Of course, gradual selling requires discipline. Without a clear plan, it's easy to fall back into the trap of procrastination or impulsiveness. That's why many sophisticated investors use tools like 10b5-1 plans to systematize their selling schedules, taking emotions—and insider trading concerns—out of the equation. Others work closely with wealth advisors to create customized liquidity calendars that blend market conditions, tax considerations, and life goals.

There are risks to consider. Selling too slowly may leave you exposed longer than is prudent. If your concentration remains high for too long, you could still suffer a large drawdown. Too fast, and you might miss significant upside or signal weakness to the market. This is why balance—tempered, strategic balance—is essential. No single formula fits everyone. Your selling strategy must be tailored to your position size, your liquidity needs, your tax picture, and your personal risk tolerance.

Another founder story: a client who resisted selling for years because "the stock always comes back." And for a while, it did. Until it didn't. When the downturn hit, she was holding 80% of her wealth in a single name. She spent the next five years rebuilding from a position of far less strength.

Contrast that with another founder who started diversifying early, even when the stock was still climbing. He missed the very top—but he protected his freedom. And freedom, not fortune, is the ultimate currency at your level.

Selling gradually isn't just a risk-management tool. It's a mindset shift. It's moving from a gambler's mentality to a steward's mentality. You're not betting your life's work on a single dice roll. You're harvesting the value you've created and redeploying it intelligently, intentionally, and sustainably.

Final Thought:

You didn't build your wealth overnight, and you shouldn't risk it overnight either. Selling gradually honors both your achievements and your future. It allows you to turn concentration into freedom without turning your back on opportunity. If you haven't yet set a gradual unwinding strategy—or if your existing plan hasn't been revisited in light of current market, tax, or regulatory conditions—it's time. Consult your advisors. Sketch the outline of a disciplined selling strategy.

Because at the ultra-affluent level, success isn't about making bold moves. It's about making wise ones.

Chapter 23: Exchange Funds, Diversifying Without Selling

If you're holding this book, chances are you've spent a lot of time weighing the cost of action versus the cost of inaction when it comes to your concentrated stock position. Sell, and you trigger capital gains. Hold, and you shoulder all the risk. It's a classic dilemma. But what if you could diversify without selling, without triggering a taxable event, and without walking away from the value you've built? Enter the exchange fund—a tool designed for people exactly like you.

Imagine this scenario: You're a founder, executive, or early employee sitting on $30 million worth of stock from your company. You believe in the company's future, but you also know the danger of putting too many eggs in one basket. You're facing significant unrealized gains, meaning a traditional sale would come with a painful tax bill. You need diversification, but you want to do it intelligently—minimizing taxes and maximizing future growth. This is where an exchange fund becomes a powerful alternative.

An exchange fund allows you to contribute your highly appreciated stock into a pooled investment vehicle alongside other investors who are in the same position. Your stock gets combined with a basket of different securities, instantly giving you exposure to a broader range of assets without selling your shares. No sale, no taxable gain. You diversify your risk profile substantially while maintaining the potential for long-term growth.

The mechanics are straightforward but sophisticated. Typically, these funds are managed by large asset managers who specialize in working with high-net-worth individuals. The fund collects stocks from dozens of participants, making sure no one company's stock dominates the portfolio. You own a pro-rata share of the overall basket, not just your original company stock. Over time—often seven years or more—you have the option to redeem your interest in the fund for a diversified portfolio of stocks.

Of course, there are important nuances to understand. Exchange funds come with lock-up periods; you generally can't pull your money out for at least seven years without facing penalties. There are also management fees to consider, and the fund's structure must comply with IRS regulations to ensure you get the intended tax deferral benefits. This isn't a casual move—it's a commitment. But for those with patience, the benefits can be remarkable.

One founder I worked with had a $50 million position in a tech company that had been life-changing but highly volatile. He was reluctant to sell and trigger a 23.8% federal capital gains tax, plus state taxes. Instead, he contributed a portion of his shares to an exchange fund. Over eight years, the diversification protected him from the rollercoaster his original company stock went through. When he exited, he had a portfolio that reflected a broad slice of the market rather than the fortunes of one volatile company.

The biggest advantage of an exchange fund is that it addresses one of the hardest problems: how to diversify without punishment. Traditional diversification—selling and reinvesting—can erode a third or more of your gains to taxes. An exchange fund allows you to defer that cost while lowering your concentration risk right away. It buys you time, diversification, and control.

But it's not perfect. If your company stock collapses before you enter the fund, you're still exposed. If the basket of stocks underperforms the market, you might not get the returns you'd hoped for. And you give up liquidity for several years. This is why a careful evaluation—looking at your liquidity needs, your risk tolerance, and your tax situation—is essential before committing.

Strategically, think of an exchange fund as one tool among many. It can work beautifully in conjunction with gradual selling strategies, 10b5-1 plans, and charitable giving vehicles like Donor-Advised Funds or Charitable Remainder Trusts. In fact, a layered approach—selling some shares while contributing others to an exchange fund—can give you even more flexibility and control.

Final Thought:

If you're sitting on substantial, concentrated stock wealth and looking for ways to unwind without triggering a tax bill or exposing yourself to single-stock risk, exchange funds deserve a serious look. They are not a magic bullet. They require thought, patience, and professional guidance. But for the right person, in the right situation, they can be a cornerstone of a smart, tax-efficient diversification strategy.

Before you make any moves, talk with your advisory team. Evaluate whether an exchange fund aligns with your liquidity needs, your tax posture, and your legacy goals. Because at this level, unwinding isn't about reacting to market swings. It's about executing a well-architected plan—one that protects not just your balance sheet, but your freedom, your influence, and your future.

Chapter 24: Collars: Hedging Risk Without Giving Up All Upside

Let's begin with a scene you may know too well: You've built a significant stake in your company, stock that has rewarded you beyond measure — but it has also tethered you tightly to its volatility. Every earnings announcement, every regulatory headline, every market correction hits closer to home than it should. You're caught in the classic dilemma: if you sell to protect yourself, you crystallize a tax event; if you hold, you remain vulnerable to the market's whims. You want protection, but you don't want to walk away from future upside. This is where a collar strategy offers an elegant solution — an advanced but underutilized way to hedge risk without sacrificing all potential gains.

A collar strategy, in its simplest form, combines two options positions. You buy a protective put option to set a floor — ensuring that if your stock price falls, you're protected below a certain level. At the same time, you sell a call option at a higher strike price — capping your maximum upside, but collecting a premium for doing so. The beauty lies in the balance: the cost of the protective put is often offset by the income from the call, resulting in little to no out-of-pocket expense. Think of it as building a fence around your wealth — not a prison, but a boundary.

Imagine this: you hold $25 million worth of a single stock. It's done well for you, but the market feels frothy, and you're not comfortable riding it unprotected. You could purchase a put option that guarantees you won't lose value below, say, $90 per share. To finance that, you sell a call option that obligates you to sell your shares if they rise above $130 per share. You've created a range — a zone of controlled outcomes. If the stock drops below $90, you're protected. If it rises above $130, you forego further gains — but in exchange, you sleep better at night, knowing your downside is managed without having to sell your stock immediately.

Collars can be particularly compelling for individuals like you — sophisticated, heavily concentrated in one equity, and navigating substantial unrealized gains. They offer a way to mitigate catastrophic loss while postponing the tax consequences of a sale. In essence, a collar helps you preserve both your wealth and your optionality — allowing you to unwind concentration risk on your terms, not the market's.

Of course, nothing is without trade-offs. By selling the call, you agree to cap your upside. If your stock skyrockets beyond the strike price of the call, you won't participate in those gains. For some, that's a frustrating ceiling. But for others, particularly those whose financial lives no longer hinge on maximizing returns but on preserving capital, the trade is more than worth it. Another consideration is the complexity of execution — collars are not DIY projects. They require careful structuring, negotiation of terms, and management of the options lifecycle.

One client, an early employee at a tech unicorn, came to me after watching his company stock climb over 600% post-IPO. He was thrilled — but increasingly nervous. He didn't want to trigger a $10 million tax bill by selling outright, but he also couldn't afford to watch the position crater. A properly structured collar provided the answer. It protected him from the worst-case downside, allowed for respectable additional upside, and bought him time. Over three years, he gradually exited his position strategically and thoughtfully, converting a once-risky concentration into a diversified, tax-efficient portfolio.

The timing of when to implement a collar matters. Ideally, you set up the strategy when volatility is relatively low, making protective puts more affordable. You also want to structure collars over periods that align with your personal liquidity needs and market outlook. In many cases, rolling collars — renewing and adjusting the strikes periodically — can give you continued protection and flexibility as markets evolve.

There's a deeper psychological benefit, too. Having a collar in place can relieve the relentless mental pressure of second-guessing your stock's every move. It allows you to shift from reactive monitoring to proactive planning. You reclaim mental bandwidth and, more importantly, the strategic advantage of making decisions based on your broader financial goals — not short-term market swings.

Strategically, collars are not a one-size-fits-all solution. They are one tool among many — best used in coordination with other strategies like 10b5-1 plans, exchange funds, charitable giving vehicles, and staged selling programs. The key is to align the collar's design with your objectives: liquidity planning, tax efficiency, downside protection, or transition timing.

If you're facing the reality of concentrated wealth and the risks it brings, a collar could be the missing piece in your strategy. It won't eliminate all the complexity, but it will give you a level of security and flexibility that pure holding or outright selling can't match. Before you act, work with experienced advisors who understand the nuances of option-based risk management. This is not about gambling with your wealth — it's about stewarding it wisely, protecting it thoughtfully, and ultimately, freeing yourself to move into the next chapter of your life and legacy on your terms.

At this stage, it's not about chasing every last dollar. It's about clarity, confidence, and control. It's about having a plan — and executing it with discipline and precision. Don't leave that to chance.

Chapter 25: Prepaid Variable Forwards, Access Liquidity Without Selling

Picture this: you're sitting on a stock position that has changed your life. It has built your wealth, it has fueled your influence — but now it's starting to feel like a gilded cage. You want liquidity. You want freedom. But selling means triggering massive taxes and losing a chunk of that carefully built capital. The irony? You're wealthier than ever on paper, but cash-poor when it comes to flexibility. It's a familiar tension for founders and early employees holding concentrated equity. And it's where a strategy like the prepaid variable forward contract — often just called a PVF — can become your best ally.

A prepaid variable forward is a financial tool designed specifically for situations like yours. In essence, it allows you to receive cash today by pledging stock for future delivery. You get liquidity without selling immediately, you defer taxes, and you retain some upside exposure. It's not a loan — there's no traditional debt to repay. Instead, you enter into a contract where you agree to deliver a certain number of shares (or cash equivalent) at a future date, typically two to five years out. The "variable" aspect means that the number of shares you ultimately deliver will depend on the stock's price at settlement — giving you partial downside protection and a cap on upside participation.

Here's a simple illustration: you own $20 million worth of a single stock. Rather than selling it and facing immediate capital gains taxes, you enter a prepaid variable forward. You receive, say, $15 million upfront — a portion of the stock's current value — and you agree to deliver shares at settlement. If the stock price drops, you benefit from downside protection. If the stock soars, you still participate in gains, but typically up to a pre-negotiated cap. In the meantime, you've got immediate liquidity — to diversify, to invest elsewhere, to fund philanthropic ambitions, or to simply sleep better knowing you're no longer tied 100% to market swings.

Real-world example: a biotech founder whose company had gone public during a volatile market cycle faced a classic dilemma. He needed liquidity to launch a family foundation and diversify his holdings, but didn't want to trigger tens of millions in taxes by selling. A prepaid variable forward enabled him to unlock over $10 million of liquidity without selling a single share — and he structured it carefully, preserving significant upside potential. When the stock later rose modestly, he still participated in gains while avoiding an immediate tax event at the time of the contract.

There are, of course, trade-offs. The PVF locks you into a future obligation — you are committed to delivering shares or settling in cash down the road. There's counterparty risk, as the contract is with a financial institution, and the terms — like floors, caps, and cash settlement options — need to be meticulously negotiated. Not every stock is suitable either — thinly traded, highly volatile stocks may not fetch favorable terms. And while you defer taxes, they aren't eliminated; the gain is recognized when the shares are delivered at settlement.

Still, for founders and executives with significant concentration and limited liquidity, the advantages are powerful. Immediate cash without immediate tax. Downside protection against major losses. Partial upside participation. And — just as importantly — time. Time to diversify at a more strategic pace. Time to plan for legacy moves like charitable giving or gifting strategies. Time to let the dust settle without being forced into reactive decisions.

One often overlooked benefit of PVFs is psychological. Liquidity can dramatically change your relationship with your wealth. Instead of feeling trapped, you feel empowered. Instead of over-monitoring your stock's price, you can think bigger: How do I deploy capital across a broader opportunity set? How do I align my wealth with my values and long-term goals? How do I protect and extend this fortune beyond my own lifetime?

Strategically, PVFs are most effective when paired with broader wealth planning. It's rarely about using just one tool — it's about coordinating PVFs with trust strategies, asset protection plans, and other liquidity solutions like exchange funds or 10b5-1 plans. Each piece needs to fit into the larger architecture of your goals, your tax picture, and your risk appetite.

As with any advanced strategy, execution matters. Partnering with sophisticated advisors — those who understand the nuance of PVF pricing, counterparty negotiation, and integration with your broader estate and investment plan — is non-negotiable. The best results don't come from chasing the biggest upfront payment; they come from aligning terms with your life strategy.

If you're sitting atop a concentrated position, rich on paper but constrained in life, a prepaid variable forward may offer a path to freedom. It's not a one-size-fits-all solution — but when used thoughtfully, it can give you back what wealth should always give you: choice. Before you rush to sell and pay the tax toll, consider whether a PVF could open a different door — one that keeps your upside, cushions your downside, and fuels your next chapter without forcing your hand.

At this level of wealth, the goal is not just to preserve your assets, but to preserve your optionality — to create a financial life that is as flexible, resilient, and intentional as the company you built. And that's the kind of wealth worth building.

Chapter 26: Charitable Remainder Trusts (CRTs): Give and Receive

If you've reached the point in your life where you're thinking about concentrated stock risk, chances are you're also thinking about the bigger picture: not just how to protect what you've built, but how to shape the legacy you leave behind. You're probably balancing two competing thoughts: the need for liquidity and the desire for impact. Charitable Remainder Trusts — CRTs — are one of the rare tools that let you do both, and they deserve a seat at your table.

A CRT is, at its core, a split-interest trust. You transfer appreciated assets — like concentrated stock — into the trust. In return, the trust pays you, or someone you choose, an income stream for life or for a term of up to 20 years. When the trust ends, the remainder goes to the charity or charities you've selected. In a single strategy, you unlock liquidity, diversify, defer or reduce taxes, and advance your philanthropic mission. Few strategies are this elegant.

Imagine a scenario: an early employee at a wildly successful tech company has accumulated $25 million in stock, with a low cost basis. Selling outright would trigger enormous capital gains taxes. Instead, she transfers $10 million worth of shares into a CRT. She receives a substantial charitable income tax deduction upfront. The trust sells the stock without paying immediate capital gains tax, reinvests the proceeds into a diversified portfolio, and pays her an annual income of 5% of the trust's value. When she passes away — or after the term ends — the remaining assets support the education foundation she helped build in her hometown. Liquidity, income, tax efficiency, and legacy — all in one move.

The tax benefits alone are powerful. First, there's the charitable deduction based on the present value of the remainder interest — often a sizable offset against your taxable income. Second, there's tax deferral: by selling inside the CRT, you avoid triggering capital gains at the time of sale. Instead, the payments you receive are taxed as you receive them, and often at more favorable rates. If you're charitably inclined, a CRT can stretch the impact of your gift significantly, leaving more for both you and your chosen cause.

But there are trade-offs to consider. A CRT is irrevocable — once you transfer assets, you can't take them back. The income payments are fixed by the trust's terms, and depending on market performance, you may not control how much your annual distribution is beyond the initial arrangement. And while the trust gives you income, it doesn't allow access to the principal once the trust is funded. In other words, it's a commitment. It's a smart move for those who know they want to weave philanthropy into their wealth strategy — but it's not for those who might need full access to their capital down the road.

Real-world example: a founder in his early 50s sold his company for a nine-figure sum. Sitting on $40 million in concentrated public stock from the acquiring company, he used a CRT to carve off $15 million. Over the next 20 years, he will receive steady income, while watching the remainder build a future endowment for his family's foundation focused on climate change initiatives. The move unlocked liquidity without the tax drag of an immediate sale and aligned his financial strategy with his broader mission.

Another key benefit of a CRT is time. It buys you breathing room — liquidity today with no forced liquidation of shares in a down market. Instead of worrying about when to sell and how much tax you'll owe, you gain a predictable income stream and let the diversified assets inside the trust grow, untouched by short-term volatility.

From a strategic planning perspective, CRTs work best when integrated thoughtfully into your overall wealth architecture. Pairing a CRT with other techniques — such as setting up a donor-advised fund to receive some of your charitable deduction spillover — can maximize flexibility. And careful coordination with your tax advisor ensures the charitable deduction is optimized to your highest income years.

Yet, perhaps the most compelling advantage of a CRT is the mindset shift it creates. Rather than viewing concentrated stock simply as a tax problem to solve, you begin to view it as a mission-enabler — a way to turn illiquidity into legacy. It's not just about what you can take from the world, but what you can give back. CRTs let you monetize success without abandoning stewardship.

Final Thought:

If you're wrestling with the risks of concentrated wealth and the pull of broader impact, a CRT may be one of the smartest bridges you can build. It turns an illiquid, risky position into a diversified, income-generating, tax-efficient, mission-driven asset. It doesn't just solve problems — it elevates possibilities. As you reflect on your next moves, ask yourself: How can I structure my liquidity not just to serve me, but to serve something larger than me? If you're ready to align your financial decisions with your future vision, the Charitable Remainder Trust might be your next great move.

At this level of affluence, good decisions don't just safeguard wealth — they amplify it, extend it, and anchor it to a purpose that endures.

Chapter 27: Donor-Advised Funds, Philanthropy Meets Tax Efficiency

One of the more overlooked, yet highly effective strategies for anyone dealing with a concentrated stock position is the use of a Donór-Advised Fund—often abbreviated as a DAF. If you're in a season of life where your concentrated equity has produced more wealth than you reasonably need, the conversation shifts from just protecting that wealth to deploying it thoughtfully. Philanthropy, when structured intelligently, can become a core pillar of both your impact and your financial strategy. And few tools allow for this blend of generosity and efficiency quite like a DAF.

Let's start by framing what a DAF actually is. A Donor-Advised Fund is a charitable investment account where you contribute assets—cash, stocks, private business interests—and receive an immediate tax deduction. The money can then be granted out to qualified charities over time, on your schedule. Think of it as your personal foundation, but with less administrative burden and more flexibility. It allows you to separate the decision to give from the decision of when and where to grant, a key advantage when you're managing timing, liquidity, and taxes.

Now imagine you're holding $20 million in a single stock position that's highly appreciated. Selling it outright would trigger substantial capital gains taxes. But transferring some of those shares into a DAF allows you to deduct the fair market value of the stock—up to 30% of your adjusted gross income—without immediately selling it yourself. The fund can liquidate the stock tax-free, and those proceeds are now ready to be granted to causes you care about, whether that's this year or ten years from now. You've avoided capital gains taxes on that portion, gained a sizable deduction, and freed yourself to be thoughtful and strategic about your giving.

The beauty of a DAF is its simplicity. You don't need to hire staff or set up a private foundation with complicated governance structures. You don't have to make complex filings with the IRS every year. The sponsoring organization handles the compliance and reporting, letting you focus on the fun part—strategic giving. For founders and executives used to moving fast, this simplicity can be a real asset.

Of course, there are nuances to consider. Contributions to a DAF are irrevocable; once you give assets to the fund, they no longer belong to you. You advise—hence the name—where grants should go, but the sponsoring organization retains legal control. However, practically speaking, they almost always follow the donor's advice unless the grant is illegal or violates their guidelines. If control and the ability to hire staff and craft mission statements are crucial to you, a private foundation might be more appropriate. But if what you seek is impact without the overhead, a DAF is a very powerful lever.

Real-world scenario: a founder who exited his SaaS company with $80 million in stock contributions faced a liquidity event triggering massive tax consequences. He contributed $10 million in stock into a DAF just prior to exit. He secured an immediate tax deduction at the pre-transaction value—substantially higher than his basis—avoiding the capital gains hit on that chunk. Over the next several years, he strategically funded educational programs, climate change initiatives, and entrepreneurship incubators, all on his timeline and under his family's guidance. His DAF became a multi-generational giving vehicle, and he avoided a significant tax hit at the point of sale.

There's also a psychological benefit to DAFs that shouldn't be overlooked. Many founders struggle emotionally with wealth, especially post-liquidity. Building a DAF early can create a sense of purpose and direction, transforming wealth from a burden into a mission. It changes the narrative from "How do I reduce taxes?" to "How can I leave a mark?" And for many high-achievers, that narrative shift is invaluable.

Another strategic layer is combining DAF funding with other techniques. You can synchronize gifts with high-income years to optimize deductions. You can even use appreciated private company shares—pending your liquidity event—with careful planning and early coordination. The earlier you start this conversation with your advisors, the more leverage you have.

But perhaps the greatest value lies in the flexibility DAFs provide. You're not rushed into quick decisions about where to give. You have time to engage your family in philanthropic discussions, to research nonprofits thoroughly, to establish a vision for your giving that feels authentic and impactful. In the fast-paced world of entrepreneurship and executive leadership, having a mechanism that buys you time while maximizing your tax efficiency is an advantage you shouldn't ignore.

If you're carrying a concentrated position and contemplating your next move, don't limit yourself to strategies focused solely on you. Think broader. Think legacy. A Donor-Advised Fund lets you pivot from reactive tax management to proactive legacy building. It transforms the act of unwinding concentration into an act of significance. Philanthropy isn't an afterthought—it's an integral part of your wealth strategy, empowering you to align your values with your assets.

The decisions you make today can fund the change you want to see tomorrow. If you're serious about impact without the bureaucracy, and serious about smartly managing your wealth, a DAF deserves your attention.

Chapter 28: GRATs and IDGTs, Estate Planning With Concentrated Stock

Let's imagine you're sitting at a familiar crossroads — substantial wealth in a single stock, either from a founding stake, early executive compensation, or a company you helped build. You've won the liquidity game, or you're close. But here's the next, harder question: How do you ensure that wealth transitions intelligently? Not just minimizing taxes, but preserving the values and vision that helped you accumulate it in the first place. At this level, simple wills and trusts don't cut it. You need tools engineered for complexity, timing, and scale. Two of the most powerful? GRATs and IDGTs.

The Grantor Retained Annuity Trust (GRAT) and the Intentionally Defective Grantor Trust (IDGT) may sound like arcane financial instruments — and to many, they are. But for you, they can become cornerstone strategies, especially when unwinding a concentrated stock position is intertwined with bigger goals: protecting your family, minimizing estate taxes, and preserving upside. Done right, they turn complexity into clarity, risk into opportunity.

Let's start with the GRAT. A GRAT is elegantly simple once you see it. You transfer assets — think your concentrated stock — into a trust that promises to pay you an annuity for a set number of years. These payments are based on an interest rate set by the IRS (the "Section 7520 rate"). If the stock appreciates beyond this assumed rate, the extra growth passes to your heirs — gift-tax free — at the end of the trust's term. The beauty of the GRAT lies in the math: if you set it up properly, the taxable gift can be almost zero, while the wealth transfer can be significant.

Now, the GRAT is not without its downsides. You have to outlive the term to realize the benefits — otherwise, the assets revert back to your estate. Additionally, if the stock underperforms the IRS hurdle rate, there's no real transfer benefit. But for founders or executives holding fast-growing shares pre-IPO, or sitting on stock that's poised for a strategic catalyst, the GRAT's leverage can be extraordinary. It's a way to push future appreciation outside your estate at very little tax cost today.

The IDGT is a different — and in many ways more nuanced — strategy. With an IDGT, you set up a trust that is "defective" for income tax purposes (meaning you pay the taxes on the trust's earnings, not the trust itself) but separate for estate tax purposes. Here's where it gets interesting: you can sell your concentrated stock to the IDGT in exchange for a promissory note. The note carries an interest rate — again, set by IRS guidelines — but if the stock appreciates faster than the interest you're owed, that excess growth stays in the trust, outside of your estate. It's another sophisticated way to "freeze" today's value for estate tax purposes and shift future gains downstream.

Real-world example: A founder, we'll call him Alex, transferred $15 million worth of pre-IPO shares into an IDGT in exchange for a 3% interest note. Five years later, his company IPO'd, and those shares appreciated to $80 million. The trust repaid the note using dividends and a small portion of shares — and the entire $65 million in appreciation passed estate-tax-free to his children. All because he took action when valuations were lower and risk/reward was in his favor.

Of course, neither GRATs nor IDGTs are silver bullets. GRATs are less flexible — you have to carefully time the term and navigate the "mortality risk" of outliving it. IDGTs require the willingness and capacity to continue paying the trust's taxes yourself, which can feel like writing checks for years without immediate personal benefit. But the trade-off — the ability to shift massive future appreciation out of your taxable estate — is a rare and potent advantage.

In both cases, the secret is timing. Setting up a GRAT or IDGT when your stock is undervalued, after a down market or before a growth catalyst, is the difference between a modest tax benefit and a generational wealth transfer. Waiting too long, until the stock is already highly valued or public, minimizes the leverage. As with so much of advanced planning, speed matters, but precision matters more.

Another key advantage of using GRATs and IDGTs with concentrated stock is the ability to pair these strategies with liquidity planning. For instance, as the GRAT or IDGT generates cash flow — through dividends, or eventual stock sales — you can reinvest in a diversified portfolio. Over time, this not only unwinds the concentration but systematically rebuilds your asset allocation, creating broader, more resilient wealth for your heirs.

It's not about trust mechanics. It's about freedom. Freedom from punitive estate taxes. Freedom to align your legacy with your values. Freedom to leave behind not just money, but stability, optionality, and stewardship for the next generation.

Final Thought:

If you're holding concentrated stock and thinking beyond just yourself — if you're planning for family, philanthropy, and legacy — it's time to think about more than selling shares. GRATs and IDGTs are not mere tax tricks. They're architectural tools for building a legacy that will last longer than your lifetime. Don't let complexity paralyze you. Assemble the right team — legal, tax, wealth advisory — and start designing your next chapter. Because at this level, true wealth isn't measured in stock certificates. It's measured in what endures.

Chapter 29: Employee Stock Options, ISOs vs. NSOs Post-Liquidity

If you've built your career — and much of your wealth — through equity compensation, you already know the tremendous power of stock options. They're the ultimate lever in a high-growth company, the tool that can transform sweat equity into real equity. But post-liquidity, after the IPO or the acquisition, options are no longer just a tool. They're a puzzle. And how you navigate that puzzle — particularly the difference between Incentive Stock Options (ISOs) and Non-Qualified Stock Options (NSOs) — can either preserve your wealth or quietly erode it.

The challenge is that most of the advice you received when you first got your options was about building wealth — how to exercise, how to hold, how to bet on your own success. Now, the conversation shifts. It's about managing concentrated exposure, optimizing tax outcomes, and translating paper wealth into enduring financial independence. And that means understanding how ISOs and NSOs behave differently once the liquidity event is behind you.

Let's start with ISOs. Incentive Stock Options were designed as a tax-favored instrument, a reward for employees to share in company growth. If you hold ISOs long enough — two years from the grant date and one year from the exercise date — you unlock long-term capital gains treatment when you sell, instead of being taxed at ordinary income rates. On paper, it sounds perfect. But here's the complication: Alternative Minimum Tax (AMT).

Exercising ISOs triggers an AMT event based on the spread between your exercise price and the fair market value at exercise. If you exercised pre-IPO at a low price, the AMT exposure might have been manageable. But if you exercised closer to the liquidity event or if you're still holding unexercised ISOs post-IPO, the spread can be enormous — and so can the AMT liability. Worse, you might face a situation where the paper value of your shares says you're rich, but the tax bill comes due before you've actually sold and realized cash. That's the ISO trap.

Contrast that with NSOs. Non-Qualified Stock Options don't offer the same favorable long-term tax treatment. When you exercise NSOs, the spread between your strike price and the fair market value is treated as ordinary income immediately, subject to payroll taxes. It's blunt, but it's clear. There's no AMT to worry about, and once exercised, you can hold the stock and benefit from long-term capital gains treatment on any additional appreciation beyond the exercise date.

Post-liquidity, ISOs and NSOs present different strategic choices. For ISOs, the clock starts ticking. You need to think carefully about whether to exercise and hold — risking AMT — or to exercise and sell quickly, converting them to a cash gain and paying short-term capital gains if you don't meet the holding period. With NSOs, the decision is simpler: exercise when you're ready to manage the income hit and diversify.

One founder I worked with had held ISOs from a tech startup that went public. After the IPO lock-up expired, she exercised all her ISOs in hopes of holding for long-term capital gains. Unfortunately, the stock fell nearly 40% within six months. Not only did she face a massive AMT bill based on the old, higher valuation, but the shares she still held were worth less than the taxes she owed. Contrast that with another client who exercised his NSOs immediately upon IPO, took the income hit, and diversified into a broad portfolio. While he paid more taxes up front, his net worth became more resilient almost overnight.

Pros and cons are everywhere in this conversation. ISOs offer the potential for better tax rates but come with AMT complexity and market risk. NSOs are simpler but guarantee a higher ordinary income tax cost. The right choice depends on your liquidity needs, your appetite for risk, and your broader financial architecture.

The key is not to let inertia make the decision for you. Many executives and founders hold on to their options too long, paralyzed by tax concerns or loyalty to the company, only to watch value evaporate. The strategic move is to build a plan. Work with your advisors — tax, legal, wealth management — to model out different scenarios. Understand what happens if you exercise now, exercise later, sell now, sell later. Look at liquidity windows, lock-up expirations, and market volatility. Timing matters more than you think.

And remember: options are a means to an end. They are not your legacy. They are not your identity. They are not your security. Their purpose is to serve the broader mission — to empower you to build durable wealth, diversified and protected, so that your impact extends far beyond a single stock or a single company.

If you're holding ISOs or NSOs post-liquidity, don't treat them as a windfall or a lottery ticket. Treat them as a complex asset that demands strategy, precision, and stewardship. Unlocking their full value means knowing when to act and when to hold. It's about intentional moves — not emotional ones. This isn't just about tax rates or timing the market. It's about mastering the transition from concentrated success to sustainable, diversified freedom. Now is the time to act — with clarity, with confidence, and with the right team by your side.

Chapter 30: Secondary Markets, Selling Private Stock Before IPO

If you've ever sat through a liquidity event waiting game — watching your net worth swell on paper but remain stubbornly inaccessible — you know firsthand how maddening private company stock can be. Especially if you're a founder, early employee, or significant shareholder, that equity can feel like both a badge of honor and a handcuff. Secondary markets were born out of that tension — offering a way to access liquidity before the IPO bell rings. Yet, as attractive as these markets are, they come with nuances, trade-offs, and complexities that are rarely discussed.

Let's start with what secondary markets actually are. In the simplest terms, they are private platforms where shareholders of pre-IPO companies can sell their stock to outside investors — usually institutional investors, family offices, or specialized funds — without waiting for the company to go public. Platforms like Forge Global, EquityZen, and Nasdaq Private Market have built sophisticated ecosystems to match sellers and buyers in these opaque waters.

Now, why do secondary markets matter for someone like you? Because concentration risk in a single company — even if it's the next tech unicorn — is real. Market timing, public valuations, regulatory delays — all can derail even the most promising IPOs. Secondary liquidity offers a release valve. It allows you to derisk gradually, unlock cash for other investments, taxes, philanthropy, or even just life without waiting for perfect market conditions.

But here's the catch: secondary transactions are not as straightforward as selling public stock. First, there's the matter of company consent. Most private companies have Right of First Refusal (ROFR) clauses embedded in their stockholder agreements, meaning they can step in and buy your shares before an outside buyer can. Some companies proactively block secondary sales to control their cap table and maintain confidentiality. Others may only allow secondary sales during specific liquidity windows. So the first step before contemplating a sale is understanding the company's policy and how it aligns with your liquidity needs.

Next, valuation. Secondary market prices are not the same as the last funding round valuation. They're negotiated — often at a discount. Buyers know they're taking on risk in illiquid, opaque assets, and they price that risk in. It's not uncommon to see discounts of 10%, 20%, even 30% to the most recent round. So while it's liquidity, it's not necessarily full value. You're trading some upside for certainty today.

The tax picture also complicates things. Depending on your holding period, the sale of private shares may trigger short-term or long-term capital gains. If you exercised options to get the shares, the clock for long-term gains doesn't start until the exercise date. And if the shares qualify as Qualified Small Business Stock (QSBS), you could be eligible for significant capital gains exclusions — but only if you meet stringent holding periods and company qualifications. In short, a secondary sale can accelerate taxes in ways that may or may not work in your favor. Coordination with your CPA is essential.

A real-world example: one founder we advised had built a sizeable position in a private SaaS company. She knew she was too exposed — nearly 80% of her net worth was tied to this one company — but the IPO was still two years away. Through a secondary transaction, she sold 25% of her shares at a 15% discount. On the surface, she left money on the table. But in reality, she locked in meaningful liquidity, diversified into real estate and municipal bonds, and positioned herself to weather whatever market volatility might arise — and as it turned out, the company's IPO got delayed, and valuations across the sector compressed.

Of course, not every founder chooses to sell early. Another executive we worked with decided to hold through to the IPO, confident the public offering would reward patience. It did — but the post-IPO lock-up crushed the stock price, and by the time he could sell, the value had dropped by more than 40%. Waiting can be a winning strategy — but it also exposes you to risks you can't control.

Strategically, think about secondary sales as a risk management tool, not a judgment on the future of your company. It's not about "giving up" on the upside. It's about managing exposure to a single, illiquid asset that — no matter how promising — carries non-trivial risks. A partial sale can provide you with flexibility and optionality while still keeping a significant stake in the company's future success.

Secondary markets are evolving, becoming more sophisticated and founder-friendly. Some companies are even building structured liquidity programs for employees and early investors to facilitate more orderly secondary transactions. If you're holding significant private company equity, it's worth exploring these markets proactively — not reactively — before urgency or market shifts force your hand.

Liquidity is freedom. And secondary markets offer a powerful, if imperfect, way to access that freedom before the traditional IPO or M&A exit. Like every tool in your wealth strategy, it's not about using it indiscriminately — it's about using it intentionally. Evaluate your concentration risk, understand your company's policies, assess your tax position, and decide if now is the right time to turn some paper wealth into real-world flexibility. Unwinding isn't about abandoning the journey — it's about making sure you control the destination.

Part IV: Tax Strategy — Keeping More of What You Earned

If building concentrated wealth takes strategy, keeping it requires even more. At the ultra-affluent level, taxes aren't just an annual nuisance — they are one of the largest single threats to preserving and growing your wealth over time. Part IV is about empowering you to think like a strategist, not a taxpayer.

This section will walk you through the nuances of how concentrated stock positions are taxed — from the moment you acquire them to the moment you exit. We'll demystify capital gains, qualified small business stock (QSBS) treatment, and the sometimes costly differences between short-term and long-term gains. More importantly, we'll explore how to time sales, structure gifts, and leverage charitable vehicles like donor-advised funds (DAFs) and charitable remainder trusts (CRTs) to strategically minimize your taxable footprint while still achieving your broader goals.

You'll also learn how tax-loss harvesting, strategic giving, estate planning structures like GRATs and IDGTs, and secondaries liquidity events can be woven into a cohesive tax plan — not just to defer taxes, but in many cases to meaningfully reduce them. Through real-world founder examples and plainspoken breakdowns of complex strategies, this section will equip you to shift from reactive tax filing to proactive tax strategy.

Because at this level, tax planning isn't just about saving money. It's about expanding the freedom and optionality that wealth was supposed to deliver. Proper tax strategy turns complexity into clarity and transforms wealth from something you have to something you can truly leverage for generations.

Chapter 31: Tax Planning Before, During, and After the Exit

Imagine standing at the top of a mountain you spent years climbing—building your business, nurturing your equity position, holding fast to your concentrated stock. You see the summit: liquidity. A chance to turn paper wealth into real wealth. But if you're not careful, much of what you've built could quietly erode away—not because of market risk, but because of taxes. And at this level, taxes are not a footnote. They are a major line item. Thoughtful tax planning before, during, and after the exit isn't a luxury; it's a necessity if you intend to preserve the wealth you've fought to create.

Let's start with a mindset shift: tax planning is not a one-time event. It's a continuum. It begins long before the wire transfer lands in your account, and it continues long after. It starts when you first imagine selling—when you still have control over timing, structure, and strategy. Waiting until the deal is signed—or worse, closed—is like waiting until after the flood to buy insurance. Proactive tax strategy can mean the difference between preserving tens of millions of dollars versus handing a disproportionate share to the IRS.

Before the exit, the focus should be on setting the foundation. Are your shares eligible for Qualified Small Business Stock (QSBS) treatment, which can eliminate up to $10 million or more in capital gains if the rules are met? Should you consider gifting shares before they appreciate further, locking in a lower valuation for gift and estate tax purposes? Are there charitable strategies—like setting up a donor-advised fund (DAF) or a charitable remainder trust (CRT)—that can offset future income while aligning with your philanthropic goals? These conversations need to happen when you still have leverage, before deals are structured and valuations are finalized.

Now, the moment of the exit itself brings its own high-stakes decisions. Here's where liquidity meets reality. The immediate temptation is to cash out and celebrate, but sophisticated founders know that how you structure your liquidity event can have long-lasting implications. Should you take a portion of the payout in stock versus cash? Should you negotiate installment payments to spread the tax impact over several years? Should you pair the liquidity event with planned sales under a 10b5-1 plan to avoid market disruption and insider trading risk? Exit strategies crafted in haste often leave tax efficiency—and money—on the table.

One real-world example underscores this. A founder exited with a $150 million windfall. Without pre-planning, he faced a $50 million tax bill in the first year alone. By contrast, another founder we advised staggered his sale across multiple years using a pre-arranged plan, layered on a charitable strategy, and successfully compressed his effective tax rate, preserving an extra $20 million in net wealth. Timing and structure matter profoundly. You control more variables than you realize—if you engage early.

But the tax story doesn't end when the deal closes. Post-exit planning is where dynasties are either built—or inadvertently dismantled. Now you face decisions about how to redeploy wealth across asset classes, how to continue tax-loss harvesting as a strategy to offset future gains, and how to use estate planning vehicles like Grantor Retained Annuity Trusts (GRATs) or Intentionally Defective Grantor Trusts (IDGTs) to shift appreciating assets out of your taxable estate.

Post-liquidity, you also have to think differently about income. Capital gains, interest, dividends—they're not just numbers anymore. They're income streams that trigger tax consequences. Careful placement of investments in tax-efficient vehicles like municipal bonds, private placement life insurance (PPLI), and carefully structured family investment partnerships can reduce annual tax drag significantly. It's about building a second act for your wealth—one where growth continues but taxes don't eat away at the compounding effect.

There's also a behavioral advantage to strategic post-exit tax planning. Having a structure in place reduces the temptation to spend impulsively or chase high-risk investments just because liquidity is abundant. It forces discipline. It forces stewardship. And it sets the tone not just for your life post-exit, but for the financial culture you pass on to future generations.

Think of tax planning like constructing a dam upstream. Done correctly, it directs the flow of your wealth where you want it to go: into investments, philanthropy, and legacy—not into government coffers. But it only works if you build it early, reinforce it consistently, and monitor it as conditions change.

So here's the call to action: If you are contemplating an exit—even if it's years away—start assembling your tax strategy team now. This is not the domain of your basic CPA or generalist attorney. You need a tax strategist who speaks exit fluently. You need a wealth advisor who understands concentration risk, liquidity planning, and multi-generational estate structuring. You need a legal team that knows how to coordinate trusts, philanthropic vehicles, and family governance.

Because unwinding concentrated stock isn't just about diversifying risk. It's about intentionally designing a future where your wealth serves your life—not the other way around. Done right, tax strategy becomes a silent partner in your success—amplifying your wealth, preserving your legacy, and unlocking the freedom you set out to achieve when you started this journey.

Now is the moment to ask: Are you ready to engineer your exit—or are you prepared to watch opportunity slip quietly through your fingers? If you're serious about preserving what you've earned, tax planning isn't optional. It's the strategy behind the strategy.

Chapter 32: Avoiding the AMT Trap with ISOs

Let's begin with a situation far too common among successful founders and early employees: you hold Incentive Stock Options (ISOs) that have grown tremendously in value. Maybe you're on the cusp of an IPO, or a liquidity event is on the calendar. You feel that swell of pride and excitement—years of sweat equity crystallizing into wealth. But lurking just beneath that optimism is a hidden trap that has blindsided even the most financially savvy individuals: the Alternative Minimum Tax, or AMT.

ISOs have always been positioned as one of the most powerful wealth-building tools for early employees and founders. Their preferential tax treatment—potentially allowing gains to be taxed as long-term capital gains rather than ordinary income—sounds perfect. But what many don't realize is that when you exercise ISOs, the spread between the exercise price and the fair market value (FMV) at the time of exercise becomes a preference item for AMT. In other words, you might owe a substantial tax bill on income you haven't actually realized yet—income that exists only on paper.

The most painful stories often come from those who exercised a large batch of ISOs right before a downturn. On paper, they were millionaires. In reality, they owed hundreds of thousands—sometimes millions—in AMT without the liquidity to pay it. And if the stock price fell before they could sell, they were left with crushing tax obligations based on a phantom gain that vanished before their eyes.

So let's be clear: AMT is not something you can afford to ignore. It demands deliberate, proactive planning. The first step is to understand your AMT exposure. This requires running mock tax returns before exercising options—not just guessing or assuming it will work out. Engage a CPA who is intimately familiar with ISO mechanics and AMT calculations. Many founders mistakenly assume their general accountant will know this; don't make that mistake.

Once you know your exposure, you can plan strategically. One smart strategy is exercising ISOs gradually over several years. By spreading out the exercise, you can potentially stay under the AMT exemption thresholds—or at least avoid catastrophic spikes. Another tactic involves exercising early in the calendar year. If things don't go as planned, and the stock price falls, you have the rest of the year to disqualify the shares from AMT impact by executing what's called a disqualifying disposition—selling the shares before year-end to trigger ordinary income treatment instead of alternative minimum taxable income.

Real-world example: one founder I worked with exercised ISOs worth $5 million in early January. By September, due to market conditions, the company's valuation dipped significantly. Because he exercised early, he still had time to sell his shares and reset the tax treatment, dramatically lowering his tax bill. Compare that to another executive who waited until November to exercise. When the market turned, he had no flexibility left—and the AMT bill came due anyway.

There's also the possibility of using an AMT credit. If you do end up paying AMT, that overpayment doesn't vanish into thin air. You can often recover it over future years as a credit against your regular tax liability. However, the recovery is slow—it can take years—and if you don't have substantial ordinary income moving forward, that credit can languish. Better to avoid overpaying in the first place.

Timing also plays a role when a liquidity event is imminent. If your company is approaching an IPO or acquisition, waiting until after the liquidity event can reset your timeline and tax strategy. But be careful: post-IPO, many companies have lock-up periods where you can't sell, and the stock's FMV will become the IPO price—likely much higher than your original grant value, intensifying AMT exposure.

Another important consideration is Qualified Small Business Stock (QSBS) treatment. In some cases, holding ISOs for the right period could make the resulting shares eligible for QSBS exclusion, allowing you to shield up to $10 million (or more, depending on structuring) from capital gains taxes entirely. Coordinating ISO exercise planning with QSBS eligibility can compound your tax efficiency dramatically—but the timelines and qualifications are strict.

The psychological challenge with AMT planning is that it feels abstract until it's painfully real. It's easy to tell yourself that exercising now is risky because you don't want to pay tax on paper gains. But risk is a double-edged sword. If you wait too long and your company's valuation skyrockets, the AMT exposure becomes even more brutal. Strategic early exercise at lower valuations can cap your risk. Think of it as paying for certainty—and reducing the future tax drag on your growing wealth.

In the end, the real message is simple: don't let AMT derail what could be the most significant wealth event of your life. Educate yourself. Run the numbers. Build a plan that integrates ISO exercise strategy with liquidity planning, tax minimization, and broader financial goals. The AMT isn't an unbeatable adversary. It's a predictable challenge for those who prepare—and a nasty surprise for those who don't.

So here's your action step: if you have ISOs and you haven't modeled your AMT exposure in the last six months—or if you're approaching a company liquidity event—schedule a consultation with a tax professional who understands the intricacies of concentrated stock and AMT. This is not a time for general advice. This is a time for precision.

Because at the end of the day, unwinding your concentrated stock position isn't just about diversifying wealth. It's about protecting what you've worked so hard to build—and ensuring the reward is worthy of the risk you took to get here.

Chapter 33: Qualified Small Business Stock (QSBS) and Section 1202

If you're holding concentrated stock and it happens to qualify as Qualified Small Business Stock—QSBS under Section 1202 of the Internal Revenue Code—you are sitting on one of the most powerful, yet least understood, tax advantages available to entrepreneurs and early employees. It's the kind of opportunity that, properly leveraged, can mean the difference between paying millions in capital gains taxes and paying nothing at all. But like all powerful tools, it comes with rules, nuances, and risks.

Let's start with a simple but high-stakes scenario: imagine you helped build a private company from its earliest days. You were granted equity when the company was valued modestly, and today it's worth a fortune. You're thinking about selling a portion post-liquidity event, and you hear from someone in your circle: "Hey, you should look into Section 1202." If you qualify, you could exclude up to $10 million—or 10 times your basis, whichever is greater—of your capital gains from federal taxes. For most founders, that could mean saving tens of millions of dollars.

But—and this is important—the clock started ticking long before you even thought about selling. To qualify, the shares must meet several stringent requirements. First, they must be original issue—meaning you acquired the stock directly from the company, not in a secondary market transaction. Second, the company itself must have qualified as a small business at the time of issuance—gross assets under $50 million, among other factors. Third, and often overlooked, you must hold the stock for at least five years. No shortcuts. If you sell even one day before the five-year mark, the QSBS benefit vanishes.

Take the real-world example of a founder I worked with recently: she exercised her options early, when the company was valued at a fraction of what it would later become. Because she was proactive, she started her five-year holding period long before the IPO. When the company went public and her lockup expired, she was able to sell $10 million in gains entirely free of federal capital gains tax. Meanwhile, a peer who delayed exercising until close to the IPO missed the QSBS window entirely—and paid millions more in taxes as a result.

Another layer to consider is the stacking strategy. There are techniques—legally sound and tested—to multiply the QSBS exclusion across multiple trusts or family members. If you have substantial concentrated wealth, it's possible to use non-grantor trusts to stack multiple $10 million exemptions. With proper planning, you're not limited to a single exclusion—you can create a tax shelter for significant generational wealth transfer.

Of course, there are traps to avoid. One common mistake is assuming your stock automatically qualifies. QSBS status can be disqualified if the company engaged in certain businesses—like professional services, finance, or hospitality—that aren't eligible under the statute. And sometimes companies inadvertently lose their QSBS eligibility by growing too large or engaging in disqualifying transactions. You can't assume; you need documentation from the company, ideally verified by your legal or tax advisor.

Timing also plays a crucial role. If you're nearing an acquisition or liquidity event and haven't met the five-year mark, there are strategies like a "rollover" under Section 1045, which can allow you to defer gains and restart the QSBS clock with a new qualified investment. But the rules are narrow, and the timeline is tight—typically 60 days to reinvest.

Another point to keep in mind is that while federal law provides this benefit, state tax treatment can vary. Some states conform to the federal QSBS exclusion; others do not. California, for example, disallowed the

QSBS benefit for many years, leading to unpleasant surprises for founders who assumed federal treatment would flow through to their state taxes.

The key takeaway here is that QSBS is not just a tax perk; it's a strategic asset. Like any asset, its value is maximized only when it's understood and actively managed. If you wait until the sale to ask about QSBS, you're too late. The planning needs to happen years before liquidity, and it should be integrated into your broader tax, estate, and investment strategies.

So what's your action step? If you think you may have QSBS-eligible shares—or even if you're not sure—get an expert review immediately. Confirm your eligibility. Start tracking your holding period meticulously. And if you're nearing a liquidity event and haven't hit the five-year mark, explore strategies like Section 1045 rollover or other creative structuring to preserve the benefit.

Unwinding concentrated stock positions demands more than just financial engineering—it demands tax mastery. And QSBS, when used wisely, is one of the most potent tax tools at your disposal. It's not just about keeping more of what you've earned—it's about honoring the years of risk and effort you invested to get here. Smart planning now means securing not just your wealth, but your legacy.

Because ultimately, this isn't just about avoiding taxes. It's about creating the freedom to reinvest in new ventures, support the causes you care about, and pass on the opportunity you built to future generations.

Chapter 34: The Net Investment Income Tax, Planning Around the 3.8% Hit

If you're sitting on a significant concentration of stock, the kind that founders, early employees, and executives often find themselves holding after years of grinding away, there's an underappreciated tax that can quietly siphon off your gains—the Net Investment Income Tax, or NIIT. Introduced in 2013, it's a 3.8% surtax that applies to investment income once your modified adjusted gross income exceeds certain thresholds. And if you're anywhere near liquidity, those thresholds aren't a concern—you're going to be paying it unless you plan proactively.

Let's walk into a real-world situation. A founder I worked with recently was preparing for a $50 million liquidity event. She'd done a great job setting up charitable vehicles, a 10b5-1 plan, and had even structured part of her holdings through a GRAT. But she hadn't factored in NIIT at all. The 3.8% might seem modest at first glance, but on $50 million, that's $1.9 million in additional tax. It's the kind of mistake that stings—especially because, with the right strategy, much of it could have been mitigated or avoided.

First, let's understand what NIIT targets. It's a tax on "net investment income"—capital gains, dividends, interest, passive business income, and certain rental income. If your modified adjusted gross income exceeds $200,000 for individuals or $250,000 for married couples filing jointly, the 3.8% NIIT applies to the lesser of your net investment income or the amount your income exceeds the threshold. For most people unwinding a large, concentrated stock position, you're well past those thresholds the minute you trigger a sale.

What's often misunderstood is that the NIIT applies in addition to capital gains tax. If you're selling long-term assets, you might already be preparing for the 20% federal long-term capital gains rate. Add the 3.8% NIIT on top, and suddenly you're facing a 23.8% effective federal tax rate before even factoring in state taxes. In high-tax states like California or New York, your total tax burden on investment gains can easily climb over 35%.

So what can you do? The key is managing your adjusted gross income and the nature of your gains. Timing matters. Spreading sales over multiple tax years through a deliberate, phased exit plan can help keep your annual gains lower, reducing the portion exposed to NIIT. Structured sales, installment agreements, or even charitable techniques like Donor-Advised Funds (DAFs) and Charitable Remainder Trusts (CRTs) can shift the taxable event or spread it out, lowering the immediate hit.

Another powerful lever is the strategic use of tax-advantaged investments. Certain forms of income—municipal bond interest, for instance—aren't subject to NIIT. While this may not solve the concentrated stock problem directly, rebalancing proceeds into tax-efficient vehicles post-exit can reduce your exposure in future years. For entrepreneurs still working through an exit, investing in Qualified Opportunity Zones is another strategy worth considering, deferring and potentially reducing future capital gains—and with it, reducing your NIIT exposure.

Trust planning also plays a critical role. Non-grantor trusts have their own NIIT threshold, which is much lower ($14,450 in 2023), but properly structured multiple non-grantor trusts can be used to distribute the concentration among several entities, each potentially qualifying for its own exemption threshold. This type of planning has to be executed carefully, and always in consultation with a qualified estate attorney and tax advisor, but it's a route many sophisticated families take.

There's a caution here, though: you don't want to let the tax tail wag the dog. Sometimes it's better to pay the 3.8% and get the diversification you need, rather than sit frozen trying to optimize every dollar. The bigger goal is financial freedom, not tax perfection. That said, smart planning can turn what would have been a mandatory surtax into a manageable or even negligible issue—freeing up more of your wealth for reinvestment, philanthropy, or legacy building.

One of the most powerful lessons from the NIIT is that wealth accumulation isn't just about what you make—it's about what you keep. Taxes like this remind us that the journey doesn't end with a liquidity event. Stewardship of wealth, at this level, requires not just intelligent asset management, but intelligent tax management.

As you consider your next steps, ask yourself: am I proactively managing my NIIT exposure, or am I sleepwalking into a seven-figure tax bill? If you're not sure, it's time to get your advisors aligned. A tax strategist working alongside your wealth advisor can ensure you're not leaving unnecessary dollars on the table.

Because in the end, every dollar saved from unnecessary taxes is a dollar that can be reinvested—into new ventures, into future generations, into the causes you care most about. Unwinding concentrated stock isn't just a financial transaction. Done well, it's the beginning of a more intentional, more powerful phase of your financial life.

Chapter 35: State Residency and Domicile Planning Before Liquidity Events

When you're on the cusp of a major liquidity event, most of the attention tends to focus on investment strategy, estate planning, or timing the sale for tax efficiency. But there's another variable that can have a dramatic impact on how much of your wealth you get to keep: where you call home. In the world of concentrated stock unwinding, state residency and domicile planning can be the difference between a massive, unavoidable tax hit—and a much more favorable outcome.

Let's start with a real story. A founder I worked with was preparing for a $100 million liquidity event. He lived in California, a state with a top marginal income tax rate hovering around 13.3%. Without careful planning, his state tax bill alone could have exceeded $13 million. The realization hit him hard—he'd focused on federal capital gains, but had underappreciated just how much state taxes would erode his net proceeds. Fortunately, we had time. He established residency in Florida—where there's no state income tax—well before the sale, significantly reducing his tax burden and saving millions.

State taxes are not an afterthought for the ultra-affluent; they are a serious financial planning variable. States like California, New York, and New Jersey are notorious for their high personal income tax rates. Meanwhile, states like Florida, Texas, Nevada, and Washington impose no personal income tax at all. Moving from a high-tax to a no-tax state in advance of a liquidity event can shift the financial outcome dramatically. But—and this is key—it's not as simple as renting a condo and getting a new driver's license. States are aggressive about tax residency audits, and they're very good at sniffing out superficial moves.

Domicile is about more than just your mailing address. It's about where your life is "centered." Revenue agencies will look at where you spend your time, where your family lives, where you vote, where you keep your valuable possessions, where your primary physician is located, where your cars are registered, and even where your pets reside. They want to know where your true home is—not just where your beach house sits. If you move states just before a liquidity event, but leave too many ties to the old state, you risk an audit and potential back taxes, penalties, and interest.

True residency planning takes time—usually 12 to 18 months ahead of a major liquidity event. That means thinking not just about the move itself, but how you document and reinforce your new domicile. Switching voter registration, changing your primary banking relationships, filing taxes in the new state, enrolling your kids in local schools, and updating estate planning documents are all critical. The goal is to leave a clear trail that supports your claim that the move was genuine, permanent, and not solely motivated by the impending liquidity event.

There are emotional considerations, too. Leaving the place where you built your company, raised your family, or contributed to the local community isn't easy. For many founders, the idea of uprooting feels like a betrayal of the journey that got them here. But thinking about domicile strategically doesn't necessarily mean abandoning your history; it's about being thoughtful with your future. Many clients maintain multiple homes and vibrant ties to their former state—they just reframe their "primary" base in a way that aligns with tax efficiency and long-term goals.

Of course, moving isn't right for everyone. If your liquidity event is imminent or the complexities of uprooting outweigh the tax benefits, there are other planning strategies—charitable contributions, trust structures, and installment sales—that can soften the tax blow. But residency planning offers a unique lever: it doesn't just defer taxes; it can outright eliminate a massive state tax liability on your capital gains.

Another common mistake is assuming you can "game" the system by spending just enough days out of state. While day-counts are important (many states use a 183-day rule), they're not the only factor. Domicile is about the total picture—your intent, your lifestyle, and your paper trail. Moving early, being comprehensive, and documenting thoroughly are what protect you from scrutiny.

Strategically, this kind of planning should always be done in concert with legal and tax advisors. Each state has its own residency standards, and the documentation requirements can be tricky. A qualified advisor can help you build the right checklist, prepare for an audit even before one happens, and ensure that your move is legally robust and defensible.

As you think about your upcoming liquidity event, ask yourself: is staying where I am worth a seven- or eight-figure tax bill? Would a strategic relocation free up more capital for reinvestment, philanthropy, or family legacy? Moving states isn't just about the tax savings—it's about aligning your financial future with the values and freedom you've worked so hard to achieve.

Because unwinding concentrated stock isn't just about risk management or diversification—it's about maximizing the rewards of your work and vision. State residency and domicile planning is one of the few levers you can pull that, when done right, creates massive, tangible value without adding risk.

Now is the time to consider whether your current domicile is aligned with your financial goals—or if a strategic move could unlock greater freedom, liquidity, and control. And remember: these decisions are best made before the liquidity moment, not after.

Chapter 36: Trust Structures to Minimize Estate Taxes

Let's begin with a reality that every ultra-high-net-worth individual must face at some point: success, especially the kind that results in a concentrated stock position, invites complexity. But the real complexity often begins after you're gone. Estate taxes — known sometimes as the "death tax" — can take a staggering toll on a large estate. And if you've spent decades building concentrated wealth, it would be a shame to see a significant portion of it siphoned off simply because the right structures weren't in place. The time to plan for that isn't tomorrow, or five years from now. It's today — before liquidity, before valuations spike, and before windows close.

Picture this: A founder with a $200 million concentrated position waits until retirement to think about estate planning. The estate tax exemption sunsets, rates creep back up, and suddenly 40% of their estate — $80 million — is slated to go to the government instead of their family or philanthropy. And that's assuming no appreciation between now and then. Waiting isn't just expensive; it's reckless stewardship. But this fate is entirely avoidable with the right trust strategies layered into your planning now.

At its core, estate planning is about control — who will benefit from your wealth, how they will benefit, and how much will be left after taxes take their bite. Trust structures are among the most powerful tools for shifting assets out of your taxable estate while preserving access, influence, or income when appropriate. For individuals with concentrated stock, these strategies can do double duty: minimizing estate taxes and unwinding concentration risk simultaneously.

One foundational structure is the Grantor Retained Annuity Trust (GRAT). A GRAT allows you to transfer appreciating assets — like concentrated stock — into a trust, while retaining an annuity stream for a set period. If the stock appreciates beyond the IRS's assumed rate (the Section 7520 rate), that excess growth passes to your heirs free of gift or estate tax. GRATs are particularly powerful in low-interest-rate environments and with volatile, high-upside assets — which describes concentrated stock to a tee. Properly structured, a GRAT can transfer significant wealth to the next generation without using up your lifetime exemption or incurring gift tax.

Then there's the Intentionally Defective Grantor Trust (IDGT). Despite the unfortunate name, this is a powerful tool. With an IDGT, you sell appreciated assets — like your concentrated shares — to the trust in exchange for a promissory note. Because the sale is to a trust you're treated as owning for income tax purposes, there's no capital gains tax on the sale itself. Future appreciation occurs outside your estate, and you "freeze" the estate value at today's lower level. Even better, because you continue to pay income taxes on behalf of the trust, it allows the trust assets to grow without erosion — a "tax burn" that is effectively an additional, tax-free gift to your heirs.

Of course, no tool is perfect. GRATs work best with assets that appreciate rapidly soon after transfer — otherwise, you might end up with no real transfer of wealth. IDGTs require careful valuation and structuring to avoid IRS challenges. And all trust strategies must be tailored carefully to balance control, access, risk, and tax efficiency. But when designed correctly, they can be transformational — turning what would have been taxable estate value into protected, generational capital.

Let me share a story. A founder I worked with had a significant position in a biotech firm. Pre-IPO, we moved shares into a two-year rolling GRAT. Over three years, as the company's valuation soared, the GRAT structure successfully transferred over $50 million to his heirs — without triggering gift taxes or using his full exemption. The key wasn't just the technical setup; it was timing, discipline, and aligning the structure with the company's growth trajectory.

Similarly, another client used an IDGT before a liquidity event. By selling a large block of pre-IPO stock to the IDGT, she froze her estate at the pre-IPO valuation. When the company went public and the stock quadrupled, all that appreciation was outside her estate — entirely escaping the 40% estate tax her heirs would have otherwise faced. That single transaction effectively saved her family over $30 million in estate taxes.

Action matters. These structures are not plug-and-play; they require coordination with estate attorneys, valuation experts, and financial advisors. And they must be executed well before a liquidity event to survive IRS scrutiny. But for founders and executives with concentrated stock, they offer a rare and powerful opportunity to transform wealth from a fleeting personal asset into a lasting family legacy.

Too many founders focus on building wealth and put off estate planning until "later." But later often comes too late. Waiting risks higher valuations, compressed timelines, less flexibility, and more aggressive IRS scrutiny. Proactivity isn't just smart — it's essential stewardship of what you've built.

If you're sitting on a large concentrated position and haven't yet explored advanced trust planning, ask yourself: what's stopping you? Is it complexity? Is it discomfort with discussing legacy? Or is it the false comfort of thinking there's still plenty of time? Legacy isn't something you build after you've exited — it's something you construct deliberately, one strategic move at a time.

This chapter is your call to action: think about how much of your wealth you want to go to the IRS — and how much you want to go to your family, your causes, your future generations. Trust structures are not just technical tools; they are your opportunity to turn today's wealth into tomorrow's impact. Stewardship isn't passive. It demands action, insight, and planning — and the time to begin is now.

Chapter 37: Asset Location, Where to Hold Different Investments

One of the subtler — but profoundly powerful — strategies in unwinding a concentrated stock position lies not just in *what* you invest in after you unwind, but *where* you hold those investments. Asset allocation — choosing the right mix of investments — gets a lot of attention. But asset location — choosing the right type of account or structure to house those investments — can quietly supercharge your after-tax returns without requiring you to take on any additional risk.

Let's start with a simple but often overlooked reality: not all income is taxed the same, and not all investments are equally tax-efficient. As a founder or early employee, you're used to thinking about wealth in terms of enterprise value and equity appreciation. Once you've diversified, though, you're entering a world where taxes on dividends, interest, short-term gains, long-term gains, and capital distributions all come into play — and the structure in which you hold these assets can dramatically affect your net outcome.

Imagine two portfolios: both return 7% annually, but one leaks 1% each year to taxes, while the other is sheltered and only leaks 0.3%. Over 20 years, that small annual difference compounds into a *massive* difference in terminal wealth. Asset location is about stopping the leak — legally and intelligently — by aligning investments with the tax characteristics of the account that holds them.

The basic principle is deceptively simple: place tax-inefficient investments

— those that generate a lot of taxable income or short-term gains — inside tax-deferred or tax-exempt accounts like IRAs or Roth IRAs. Meanwhile, place tax-efficient investments — like municipal bonds or long-term growth equities — in taxable accounts. Why? Because you want to minimize taxable distributions where you can't defer or shelter them and maximize them where you can.

For example, consider holding high-turnover mutual funds, high-yield bonds, or REITs inside a traditional IRA. These assets often generate regular income or short-term capital gains, which are taxed at ordinary income rates — but inside an IRA, you defer the tax hit entirely. On the other hand, low-turnover index funds, tax-managed funds, or direct holdings in individual stocks — especially those you intend to hold for long periods — are better candidates for taxable accounts, where you can benefit from long-term capital gains treatment and step-up in basis at death.

Now, for those unwinding concentrated stock, this becomes even more strategic. You might harvest gains gradually over several years to manage tax brackets. But once you redeploy that capital, deciding where to place each new investment can significantly alter your long-term effective tax rate. Building tax efficiency into your reallocation plan is just as important as deciding what new assets to buy.

Here's a founder-level case study: One client exited a large concentrated position post-IPO and faced the common conundrum — massive liquidity, massive taxable events ahead. Working closely with their advisory team, they not only diversified the proceeds but carefully matched each asset class to the right location. Private credit funds went into IRAs; growth equities sat in taxable accounts; municipal bonds were used to manage after-tax income needs. Over 10 years, the tax drag on their portfolio was 30% lower than if they had ignored asset location altogether. That translated into millions of dollars in additional net worth — without taking a single additional dollar of investment risk.

Of course, this strategy isn't without nuance. IRAs and other tax-deferred accounts come with their own rules — required minimum distributions (RMDs), potential early withdrawal penalties, and limits on contributions and conversions. Roth IRAs offer the powerful benefit of tax-free growth and withdrawals, making them ideal for the most aggressive, high-growth assets you want to shield for decades — but getting assets into Roth accounts can require careful planning, especially given income limits and contribution caps.

Asset location is also dynamic. Tax laws change. Your personal situation evolves. Your portfolio mix shifts. That's why asset location isn't a one-time decision — it's an ongoing discipline, reviewed at least annually, and adjusted as needed to ensure continued alignment with both tax policy and your broader financial plan.

The key takeaway is that asset location can be just as valuable, if not more so, than chasing higher returns. It's about efficiency, discipline, and maximizing what you keep — not just what you earn. And the earlier you integrate it into your diversification strategy, the more compounding works in your favor over time.

As you unwind your concentrated stock position and shift into broader portfolio construction, don't let asset location be an afterthought. Incorporate it into your strategy from the start, and let it quietly but powerfully enhance your long-term financial freedom.

This chapter is your invitation to move from merely *investing* to *intelligently positioning* your wealth. Don't leave money on the table simply because you parked the right investment in the wrong account. Take action: review your asset location strategy today — or, better yet, build it deliberately as you unwind your concentration and embark on your next chapter of wealth stewardship.

Chapter 38: Capital Gains Harvesting vs. Loss Harvesting

When we talk about unwinding a concentrated stock position, taxes are inevitably part of the conversation. But it's not just about minimizing taxes — it's about *managing* them wisely. And that brings us to a sophisticated pair of strategies that many ultra-high-net-worth individuals overlook: capital gains harvesting and tax-loss harvesting. Understanding both — and when to deploy each — is a key lever in not just reducing taxes today but optimizing your long-term financial position.

Let's start with tax-loss harvesting. This is the more familiar of the two. At its core, it's the practice of selling an investment at a loss to offset realized gains elsewhere in your portfolio. Losses can offset gains dollar for dollar, and if you have more losses than gains, you can use up to $3,000 per year to offset ordinary income, carrying forward the rest. For someone unwinding a concentrated stock position, loss harvesting can soften the tax hit when selling appreciated shares. Done well, it creates a kind of "tax asset" that reduces your tax bill without materially altering your overall investment exposure — often achieved by swapping into similar but not "substantially identical" securities to avoid wash-sale rules.

Now, capital gains harvesting might sound counterintuitive. Why would you *realize* a gain deliberately, and voluntarily trigger a tax bill? The answer lies in tax bracket management and long-term planning. For instance, in years when your income is unusually low — say, after stepping down from an operating role but before large capital infusions from asset sales — you might fall into a lower capital gains tax bracket. If you can realize gains at a 0% or 15% federal rate rather than 20% or more later, harvesting those gains strategically locks in appreciated value at a much lower tax cost.

Consider the founder who exited operational duties but still held a large block of stock. For the few years before a full liquidity event, his ordinary income plummeted — creating a window where his capital gains could be harvested at favorable rates. Instead of waiting for an inevitable sale under high-income conditions, he began selling shares gradually, soaking up the lower tax brackets each year. Over time, the cumulative tax savings exceeded seven figures.

But harvesting gains isn't only about tax rates — it's also about resetting cost basis. Selling appreciated assets now and repurchasing them (where permitted) resets the purchase price higher, which can reduce future taxable gains and create greater flexibility for later strategic moves, such as gifting or estate planning. In essence, you're pre-paying tax today at favorable rates to reduce exposure tomorrow.

The decision between loss harvesting and gains harvesting is situational — it depends on your current income, your anticipated future income, market conditions, and your broader liquidity needs. One is defensive (loss harvesting), protecting against tax bills triggered by selling appreciated assets. The other is opportunistic (gains harvesting), taking advantage of temporarily favorable tax conditions or market declines to reset cost basis or lock in gains.

Pros and cons exist for both approaches. Loss harvesting is generally less controversial — who wouldn't want to capture deductions? But it can inadvertently lead to poor investment behavior if you start focusing more on tax deductions than portfolio quality. Gains harvesting, on the other hand, demands cash or liquidity to pay the tax bill and risks seeming aggressive — but if timed well, it is a tool of the patient and the strategic, not the impulsive.

One trap to avoid: don't let the tax tail wag the investment dog. If an asset no longer fits your risk profile or your broader financial goals, selling — and managing the taxes as a secondary step — is almost always better than holding on just to avoid a taxable event. Both loss and gains harvesting are tools, not end goals.

Another important consideration: you can blend these strategies. For instance, you might harvest losses from underperforming investments to offset gains from selling concentrated stock. Simultaneously, you could harvest gains from assets where you have the opportunity to lock in long-term capital gains at a favorable rate. This requires sophisticated modeling and scenario planning — but for UHNW individuals, the payoff is material.

The call to action here is clear: review your tax positioning not just at year-end, but throughout the year. Work with advisors who understand not only investment management but proactive tax strategy. The best time to plan harvesting strategies is long before you're forced to act.

Unwinding your concentrated stock is a major milestone — but it's also a major opportunity. Intelligent harvesting strategies — both of gains and losses — are how you maximize the after-tax value of what you've built. Managing taxes proactively isn't about paying less just for the sake of it — it's about buying more freedom, more flexibility, and more control over your financial future.

Chapter 39: Why Tax Deferral Can Be More Powerful Than Tax Minimization

When most people think about taxes, especially in the context of concentrated stock, the natural instinct is to minimize, minimize, minimize. Slash the bill now. Find every deduction. Deploy every strategy to pay as little as possible today. That's understandable — taxes can feel punitive, especially after years or decades of hard work. But as your financial life evolves from simple accumulation to complex stewardship, the goal changes. Sometimes, minimizing today's taxes is not the smartest move. Sometimes, *deferring* taxes — postponing the liability — can be far more powerful in the long arc of building, preserving, and transitioning wealth.

Let's break this open with a simple truth: time is the most underappreciated asset in tax strategy. Deferral lets your wealth grow undisturbed. Instead of giving up a slice of your investment gains to taxes today, you keep the full pie compounding, potentially for years or even decades. That compounding on untaxed gains can dramatically outpace the benefits of small, incremental tax savings today.

Imagine two founders. One liquidates their concentrated stock aggressively, paying the taxes up front to "get it over with." The other founder defers, carefully structuring their sales, perhaps using exchange funds, installment sales, or charitable remainder trusts. Ten years later, the second founder hasn't just saved taxes — they've kept more capital compounding longer. Their net worth isn't just marginally higher; it's meaningfully larger because the dollars that would have gone to taxes continued to grow.

It's a paradox worth pausing on: sometimes the way to keep more is not by cutting the tax bill down, but by delaying when you pay it. Tax deferral strategies recognize the power of opportunity cost — what you lose not just in taxes paid, but in growth potential surrendered by paying too soon. By deferring taxes, you retain control over the capital and the timing of your liabilities.

Of course, deferral isn't without risks. Markets are volatile. Tax laws can change. Deferral strategies must be managed carefully, with an eye toward legislative shifts and liquidity needs. But done well, the long-term advantages can eclipse even the most aggressive short-term minimization tactics. It's not about avoiding taxes forever — it's about paying them later, smarter, and in a more controlled environment.

There's another powerful benefit to tax deferral: flexibility. When you defer taxes, you maintain more options. You can match gains to low-income years, time large charitable gifts for maximum impact, or strategically transfer wealth to family members or trusts when it's most efficient. Immediate minimization tends to lock you into decisions; deferral preserves optionality.

Take the founder who used a series of 10b5-1 plans to unwind stock gradually over years instead of all at once. By layering sales over time, they managed their tax brackets and even accelerated charitable giving during peak earnings years to capture maximum deductions. They didn't eliminate taxes — they orchestrated them.

Or consider the entrepreneur who moved to a state with no income tax before a planned liquidity event. The federal taxes didn't go away, but by deferring the event until after changing domicile, they avoided a substantial state tax bite. This wasn't tax evasion — it was strategic tax planning made possible by deferral.

That's the true goal here: mastery, not reaction. Deferral is a tool of patience and foresight. It's a strategy that respects the complexity of your life and recognizes that the best outcomes often come not from racing to the finish line, but from carefully controlling the journey.

Here's your call to action: step back and evaluate your tax planning lens. Are you focused solely on minimizing the bill this year? Or are you building a strategy that uses time as an ally, not an enemy? In concentrated stock planning, the decision to defer — when appropriate — could be the most powerful wealth-building lever you haven't yet pulled.

Because real wealth mastery isn't just about what you earn. It's about what you keep working for you, as long and as efficiently as possible. And sometimes, keeping it working means deferring the day the tax collector knocks on your door.

Chapter 40: Coordinating with Your CPA, Attorney, and Wealth Advisor

When you built your company, you didn't do it alone. You had a team — key employees, mentors, partners — and success came not just from what you knew, but from how well you orchestrated the people around you. Unwinding a concentrated stock position isn't much different. It's not a solo project. It requires a carefully coordinated team: a CPA who understands the intricacies of tax timing, an attorney who can structure vehicles to protect your wealth, and a wealth advisor who sees the broader landscape and keeps all the moving parts in motion. The difference between a fragmented, stressful process and a smooth, strategic execution often comes down to how well you integrate your team.

Let's start with why coordination matters. Your CPA sees the world through a tax lens — minimizing liabilities, optimizing deductions, structuring gains and losses. Your attorney views it from a legal and asset protection perspective — trusts, liability shields, succession planning. Your wealth advisor focuses on the investment side — diversification, liquidity, risk management. Individually, they're each vital. But only together can they build a plan that's cohesive. A siloed team leaves gaps; a coordinated team builds resilience.

For example, imagine selling a large block of stock without consulting your CPA first. You might trigger an unexpectedly large tax bill, miss out on deferral strategies, or even stumble into AMT exposure if stock options are involved. Or think about setting up a trust with your attorney without discussing asset allocation or liquidity needs with your advisor — you could end up locking up assets in ways that hurt your overall portfolio flexibility. Coordination isn't just helpful; it's essential.

The best teams are proactive. They don't wait for problems to arise — they anticipate them. They run mock scenarios: What happens if you sell now versus in six months? How would a shift in tax law impact your exit strategy? How do family dynamics play into ownership transfers? Proactive collaboration means better modeling, smarter sequencing, and fewer unpleasant surprises.

It also matters how you position yourself with your team. You're the CEO of this process. Your advisors are not separate departments — they're your C-suite. Just as you'd expect your COO, CFO, and CTO to work together for the good of the company, you should expect — and demand — collaboration among your financial team. Set the tone early. Make it clear that no major move happens without everyone in the loop. Insist on regular joint meetings, not just siloed updates.

Real coordination means more than email threads. It means strategic planning sessions where everyone brings their expertise to the table, where risks are identified early, and where everyone is working toward the same goal — protecting and maximizing your wealth. It's one thing to have a great CPA, a sharp attorney, and a savvy advisor. It's another to have them acting as a true team.

One of the key benefits of this coordination is better sequencing. When you unwind concentrated stock, timing matters. The order of transactions — which assets are sold, gifted, or transferred first — can dramatically impact your tax bill, your liquidity, and your estate plan. A good CPA might know the tax impacts. A good advisor might know how to redeploy proceeds. But only together can they craft the best sequence that minimizes taxes, maximizes liquidity, and aligns with your legacy goals.

Let's not ignore the emotional side either. Wealth decisions are rarely purely logical. They're layered with family dynamics, legacy concerns, and personal identity. A coordinated team provides a buffer. They can bring objective perspectives, helping you navigate decisions that feel overwhelming or fraught. They can remind you of your bigger mission when the temptation is to act on short-term fear or excitement.

Here's a real-world example: a founder preparing for a large liquidity event wanted to create a charitable foundation but wasn't sure about timing. His attorney suggested waiting until after the sale, but the CPA pointed out that pre-funding a donor-advised fund before the sale could offset a significant portion of the taxable gain. Meanwhile, the wealth advisor structured a post-sale investment strategy to ensure liquidity for the foundation's giving plan. Individually, each piece was solid. Together, they created a masterstroke — a plan that optimized taxes, fulfilled personal philanthropic goals, and maintained financial flexibility.

Your call to action is this: Look at your team right now. Are they operating in silos, or are they working together? Are you leading them like a CEO, or are you passively receiving fragmented advice? Demand more. Convene them. Clarify the mission. Build the playbook together. Because at this level, success isn't about one good decision. It's about the coordination of many smart moves, executed in harmony.

Unwinding concentrated stock is one of the highest-stakes maneuvers you'll ever execute. You wouldn't bet your company on an uncoordinated team — don't bet your legacy on one either.

Part V: Building the Next Chapter — Life After Concentration

Unwinding a concentrated stock position isn't just a financial transaction — it's a profound transition. After years, perhaps decades, of wealth tied to one asset, one company, one identity, the liquidity event marks the start of an entirely new chapter. Part V is about what comes next — and how to approach it with the same purpose and precision that built your success.

In this section, we shift the conversation from dismantling risk to designing freedom. We explore how to redefine your relationship with wealth once it's no longer tied to a single entity. We'll dive into strategies for redeploying capital intentionally, aligning investments with values, and protecting your new financial architecture for the long term. We'll also confront the emotional and psychological shifts that often accompany sudden liquidity — identity recalibration, redefining purpose, and the sometimes unexpected complexity of newfound freedom.

Expect to build a vision for what comes after diversification: sustainable wealth management, family legacy cultivation, and meaningful philanthropy. We'll examine how to engineer structures that support multigenerational resilience rather than short-term consumption. You'll learn how to maintain the discipline that got you here, even when the traditional motivators — growth targets, exit milestones — are no longer front and center.

Most importantly, Part V will challenge you to lead not just your portfolio, but your life, with clarity and intention. Because the goal isn't merely to unwind concentrated stock — it's to unlock a future that's bigger, freer, and more impactful than anything that came before.

Chapter 41: Redefining Wealth, Freedom, Not Just Numbers

When you've spent decades building value — in a company, a brand, an idea — it's easy to let wealth become synonymous with numbers. Revenue milestones, valuations, cap tables, net worth calculators — these were the metrics that shaped your professional life. But the act of unwinding concentrated stock invites a deeper question: What is wealth really for? Once you're past the liquidity event, past the spreadsheets and the headlines, what remains? The answer, for those ready to listen, is simple and profound: wealth isn't about numbers — it's about freedom.

Freedom is an elusive concept in the founder's world. For years, perhaps decades, you were tethered — to investors, to a board, to customers, to employees. Even your personal net worth was tied up in the future success of one entity. Risk wasn't something abstract — it was baked into your everyday existence. Now, with liquidity, that tie is finally cut. And yet, if you're not careful, you'll replace one tether with another — tying yourself to markets, to benchmarks, to fleeting definitions of "success" measured in decimals and percentages.

This is the quiet trap that ensnares many who successfully unwind concentration. They move from business KPIs to portfolio KPIs, from equity grants to quarterly reports. They exchange entrepreneurial risk for market risk, and they chase alpha the same way they once chased Series A funding. But true freedom doesn't live in performance metrics. True freedom lives in the ability to say no. To chart your course without fear. To design a life not dictated by volatility, but by values.

Let's pause here: this is not an argument against discipline or intentional wealth management. On the contrary, discipline is what unlocks true freedom. But discipline must be aligned with purpose. Without it, you risk building a larger, more gilded cage — one that looks impressive from the outside but feels just as confining as the startup grind you thought you escaped. Real wealth, properly stewarded, expands your options. It doesn't imprison you with new obligations.

Many ultra-affluent individuals find themselves unprepared for this next phase because they never reframed their definition of wealth. They think they need to keep winning at the same game — bigger returns, bigger deals, bigger assets. But the game has changed. Now, the real victory is different. It's autonomy over your time. It's control over who you spend your days with. It's permission to prioritize meaning over motion, depth over speed, impact over income.

Consider a founder who sold his tech company for a nine-figure sum. For years, his calendar was jammed with meetings, pitches, and endless travel. Post-liquidity, he fell into the pattern many do — diving into angel investments, SPACs, private equity deals. It took him a few years to realize that he wasn't happier — just busier. It wasn't until he reframed his definition of wealth — viewing it as the fuel for personal and philanthropic freedom — that he found peace. He stopped chasing deals. He started chasing days that aligned with his values. He invested time in his family, his passions, and causes he believed in. His wealth didn't shrink. His fulfillment expanded.

This is the pivot you're invited to make. Post-concentration, your job is no longer just wealth accumulation — it's wealth activation. How can your resources create a richer life, not just a larger balance sheet? How can you steward what you've built into something that sustains not just your financial goals, but your human goals — relationships, experiences, impact?

Strategically, this means designing an investment portfolio that matches your desired life, not someone else's benchmark. It means clarifying what "enough" looks like — and having the courage to walk away from opportunities that threaten your time, sanity, or relationships. It means saying no to endless more — and yes to what matters most. Financial planning at this stage is life planning in disguise.

There are, of course, tools to support this. Trust structures that free your heirs from entitlement. Philanthropic vehicles that let you give with joy and efficiency. Investment strategies that prioritize sustainable, tax-efficient income over flashy, high-risk bets. But these are tactics. They work best when they are in service of a bigger strategy: a strategy to protect and maximize your freedom.

So here's your challenge: sit with the question most people never ask. What does freedom mean to you? If it's not about more, what is it about? And are your financial decisions — today, right now — moving you closer to that definition, or further away?

Because unwinding concentrated stock is not the end of the road. It's the beginning of a new journey — one where the real measure of wealth is not how much you have, but how well you live.

Chapter 42: Financial Literacy for the Next Generation

One of the more sobering moments after a major liquidity event is realizing that you have not just secured your own future, but altered the trajectory of your family for generations. With that shift comes an enormous responsibility — one that many ultra-affluent families overlook until it's too late. The money will outlive you. The question is whether the wisdom will. In this new chapter of your life, transferring financial literacy to the next generation becomes as critical as transferring assets.

It's tempting to assume that wealth will self-perpetuate, that the structures you've built will protect future generations from financial missteps. Trusts, governance documents, carefully drafted estate plans — these are vital. But documents alone can't teach judgment. They can't instill values. They can't prepare your heirs to be stewards rather than spenders. Without intentional education, what you've worked a lifetime to build can erode in just a few decades. The family that doesn't learn together often loses together.

Financial literacy, at this level, isn't about teaching your children how to balance a checkbook or budget their first paycheck — though those skills are important early on. It's about helping them understand the concepts of risk, return, diversification, taxes, and compounding in a way that connects to their lives and their futures. It's about cultivating a mindset of stewardship, not entitlement. Of empowerment, not dependence.

Let's be honest — money complicates relationships. It adds layers to family dynamics that are already delicate. Introducing financial literacy into the conversation requires care, strategy, and patience. It's not a one-time seminar or a quick conversation at the dinner table. It's a series of ongoing, progressive discussions, tailored to your children's age, maturity, and life stage. Start with values: what does money mean in your family? What is it for? What is it not for?

A real-world example: a founder who exited her company for several hundred million dollars began introducing her teenage children to family financial meetings. Not to lecture them, but to expose them. She brought them into conversations about the family foundation, encouraged them to propose grants, and asked them to present ideas for how they would manage a small investment portfolio. It wasn't perfect — sometimes it was awkward — but it planted seeds of responsibility and curiosity. Seeds that grew into capability.

Contrast that with another family — equally successful financially — who kept their children in the dark out of a desire to protect them. When the family patriarch passed away unexpectedly, the heirs inherited not just wealth, but confusion. Unfamiliar with basic investment principles, tax implications, or even the family's broader mission, they became targets for bad advice and poor decisions. The outcome wasn't just diminished wealth — it was fractured relationships.

There's a profound difference between transferring assets and transferring wisdom. One preserves numbers; the other preserves legacy. At this level, you must actively decide what kind of legacy you want to leave — and that means being proactive. Arrange for education — formal or informal. Bring in outside advisors to teach workshops on investing, taxes, estate planning. Foster an environment where asking questions about money isn't taboo, but expected. Make financial literacy a family tradition.

There are real tactical strategies to help here. Gradually introduce trust structures and investment accounts under their stewardship, with guardrails. Create family mission statements that connect wealth to purpose. Encourage philanthropic initiatives where younger generations can participate actively, learning not just how to give money away, but how to think about impact and sustainability. The goal isn't just competence — it's confidence and clarity.

Ultimately, the best financial literacy plan is one that empowers the next generation to view wealth not as a lottery ticket, but as a responsibility. They should understand that the wealth you're passing on is not the end of their journey, but the beginning of their own. Their job isn't to preserve the balance sheet; it's to preserve and expand the values, the vision, and the opportunities that wealth can support.

So here's your next step: reflect on your own financial education. What do you wish someone had taught you earlier? What mistakes cost you time, stress, or money? Commit to sharing that wisdom with your family. Create a plan — not just for wealth transfer, but for knowledge transfer. Because in the end, financial literacy isn't just about building wealth. It's about building lasting freedom, stewardship, and legacy — the kind of wealth that endures long after the spreadsheets are forgotten.

Chapter 43: Creating a Family Investment Policy Statement (IPS)

One of the most overlooked — yet most powerful — tools in preserving family wealth across generations isn't a portfolio allocation or a trust structure. It's clarity. And that clarity often comes in the form of a Family Investment Policy Statement (IPS). At your level of wealth, strategy without structure is a recipe for drift. Over time, drift turns into dysfunction — not just in the portfolio, but in the family. An IPS isn't just a document for investment managers. It's a tool for creating shared understanding, purpose, and discipline across the entire family enterprise.

Think of the IPS as the family's constitution when it comes to money. It articulates not just what you're investing in, but why you're investing. It sets the rules of engagement. It defines success. It establishes boundaries. And most critically, it prevents knee-jerk decisions that tend to arise when markets are volatile, or when family dynamics become, inevitably, complicated. A well-constructed IPS transforms emotional, reactionary conversations into strategic, thoughtful ones.

You might wonder: "Why do we need another document when we already have advisors?" Because advisors — no matter how good — can only work as effectively as the instructions they've been given. Without a unified vision, you'll find yourself with a fragmented portfolio, a disjointed approach, and conflicting voices pulling the strategy in different directions. Worse, when the next generation becomes involved, the absence of a clearly articulated investment philosophy can create confusion, resentment, and ultimately, wealth destruction.

A good IPS starts with values. What matters to your family? Is it wealth preservation? Growth? Philanthropy? Entrepreneurship? These priorities influence everything that follows — from asset allocation to risk tolerance to liquidity needs. Without alignment on these fundamentals, even the most technically sound investment plan will falter. It's not enough to chase returns; you need to anchor the portfolio to your family's unique goals and identity.

Real-world example: a family exited a successful business and received a significant liquidity event. Without a policy in place, the siblings inherited equal ownership in a diversified portfolio — but wildly divergent expectations. One wanted aggressive growth; another wanted income; a third wanted to divest entirely and focus on impact investing. The result? Gridlock. Arguments. Lost time and trust. Now contrast that with another family who built an IPS in advance, articulating their shared philosophy: 60% of assets aimed at generational growth, 30% at stability and income, 10% earmarked for mission-driven investing. Clear rules. Clear governance. Clear peace of mind.

The IPS should also codify risk tolerance and capacity. It's one thing for an individual to say they're comfortable with volatility. It's another for a group of heirs, spouses, and advisors to navigate a market downturn without panic. A strong IPS anticipates stress scenarios — market crashes, interest rate spikes, liquidity crunches — and lays out in advance how the family will respond. That kind of foresight removes the emotion from future decision-making.

Another critical component: rebalancing policies. Without them, portfolios become victims of their own momentum. Gains aren't captured; risks aren't trimmed; discipline erodes. A well-structured IPS specifies how and when rebalancing happens, keeping the strategy intact even when emotions run high. It's automated discipline — and at this level, discipline compounds just as powerfully as capital.

You should also address delegation. Who has authority to make investment decisions? Who must be consulted? What thresholds trigger review or approval? By formalizing these roles, you avoid future power struggles and maintain operational clarity. Advisors appreciate it. So will your heirs. Ambiguity breeds conflict. Clarity breeds continuity.

Finally, remember: the IPS isn't a static document. It's a living guide. Review it annually. Update it as circumstances evolve — births, deaths, liquidity events, new philanthropic goals. The world will change. Your family will change. Your strategy must evolve with them. But the anchor — the principles — should remain steady.

If you don't have an IPS, the next step is clear: schedule a meeting with your advisors and begin drafting one. If you do have one but haven't reviewed it recently, make it a priority. Invite your family into the process. Let it be an opportunity for dialogue, not just documentation. Because the goal here isn't just to protect wealth. It's to protect relationships. To preserve harmony. To ensure that the wealth you've built becomes a platform for empowerment — not division.

Wealth stewardship isn't about dictating from the grave. It's about laying the groundwork for generations to thrive. And at the center of that stewardship lies clarity. The IPS is your blueprint. Build it thoughtfully. Update it deliberately. And trust it to guide you when the storms come — because they will.

Chapter 44: Balancing Growth, Preservation, and Impact

At this stage in your wealth journey, the stakes are no longer about survival or even simple success — they're about balance. You've built substantial wealth through concentration, discipline, and a healthy dose of conviction. But post-concentration, the strategy shifts. It becomes less about maximizing returns at all costs and more about calibrating between three powerful, competing forces: growth, preservation, and impact.

Growth is the instinct that likely got you here. It's wired into founders, executives, and early employees. The drive to build, scale, and capture upside is what created the concentrated position in the first place. Yet post-liquidity, unchecked growth strategies often carry hidden risks. Public market volatility, private market illiquidity, macroeconomic shifts — all can erode wealth if growth is pursued without a parallel focus on preservation. Growth, for your new chapter, must be strategic — not speculative.

Preservation, meanwhile, is the new seatbelt. At first glance, preservation strategies can feel uninspiring: municipal bonds, high-quality equities, diversified real assets. But the objective has changed. Now, the goal is not just to make more — it's to protect what already exists. Preservation is what ensures the wealth you've built continues to serve you and future generations. It's what allows you to endure market cycles without losing sleep — and without sacrificing your larger ambitions.

Impact is where wealth transcends balance sheets. Whether through direct philanthropy, mission-aligned investing, or building an operating legacy, impact gives wealth a purpose beyond the self. It's no coincidence that many ultra-wealthy individuals, after unwinding concentrated wealth, find fulfillment not in higher returns, but in shaping their communities, industries, and futures in ways that outlast them. Impact, when integrated thoughtfully, can exist alongside — not in opposition to — growth and preservation.

The art, of course, is in balancing these three forces. Too much growth and you expose yourself to volatility that could wipe out decades of work. Too much preservation and you risk underperforming inflation and losing purchasing power. Too much focus on impact, without sound financial planning, and you may unintentionally limit your ability to sustain giving or investment in future generations.

Real-world example: A founder who sold their tech company for $500 million faced this exact dilemma. Their initial instinct was to continue investing heavily in high-growth startups — replicating the playbook that had worked before. But a disciplined advisor helped reframe the strategy: one-third allocated to a growth-oriented but diversified portfolio, one-third to preservation vehicles including real assets and municipal bonds, and one-third earmarked for direct philanthropic ventures and a donor-advised fund. This structure gave them permission to pursue growth without endangering their financial base and allowed impact to become a living, breathing part of their wealth — not just a line item on a charitable contribution form.

Building that balance starts with asking the right questions: What are you optimizing for now — and for whom? What portion of your wealth must be inviolable to guarantee personal security, family legacy, or future opportunities? How much risk do you need to take — not just how much risk can you tolerate? And what impact do you want your wealth to have, not just during your lifetime, but long after?

There's no one-size-fits-all formula. Some families find that 60% growth, 30% preservation, and 10% impact works for them. Others may shift to 50-30-20 depending on personal values and liquidity needs. The ratios matter less than the intentionality behind them. Without a framework, every market move feels like a crisis; with a framework, volatility becomes a data point, not a disruption.

One action step to take: carve out time — ideally with your advisory team — to sketch out what your own personal "Wealth Allocation Statement" would look like. Not just your asset allocation across stocks and bonds, but your life allocation across growth, preservation, and impact. Document it. Stress test it. Update it as life evolves.

Because ultimately, wealth is a tool. Not an end in itself, but a means to build freedom, security, and significance. Balancing growth, preservation, and impact isn't just good portfolio construction. It's good life construction.

Unwinding your concentrated stock position is the beginning of this next chapter. Balance is what will allow you not just to protect the wealth you've earned — but to deploy it in ways that bring meaning, stability, and legacy into sharp, lasting focus.

Chapter 45: Setting Up Your Family Office: When and How

There's a moment in many wealth journeys when the game changes. Success creates a complexity that no longer fits neatly inside a brokerage account or a few trust documents. Suddenly, the demands of your wealth — investments, taxes, estate planning, philanthropy, risk management, family education — feel like running a business. And like any business, complex wealth needs structure, leadership, and strategy. That's where a family office enters the conversation.

Setting up a family office isn't just about prestige — it's about necessity. It's about taking the fragmented pieces of your financial life and building a cohesive enterprise around them. It's about replacing a scattered team of individual advisors with an integrated strategy, one that ensures every decision — investment, tax, philanthropic — moves in concert toward your family's vision. But the key question is: when does a family office make sense, and how do you build one right?

The "when" usually arrives when wealth crosses a certain complexity threshold. It's not strictly about a dollar amount, but most experts suggest that managing north of $100 million in investable assets is where the economics begin to tilt in favor of a dedicated family office structure. But the real marker is not a net worth figure — it's complexity. Multiple generations, operating businesses, trusts across jurisdictions, sophisticated investment strategies, philanthropy, tax optimization — when these needs stack up, coordination demands a dedicated team.

Take the example of a founder who, post-liquidity, was managing $350 million in assets, 11 trusts, three private foundations, and investments spanning real estate, private equity, and venture capital. His life had become a tangle of quarterly calls, tax surprises, and uncoordinated advice. Transitioning to a family office brought focus and efficiency. With an in-house CFO, legal counsel, and investment director, he no longer managed the pieces — he managed the strategy.

As for the "how," it starts with defining scope. Family offices come in many shapes and sizes. Some are lean — a few trusted professionals handling accounting, investment oversight, and legal coordination. Others are robust — complete with investment committees, private equity teams, philanthropic advisory groups, even family education directors. The structure should match the complexity and ambitions of your wealth. Overbuild, and you waste resources; underbuild, and you risk costly gaps.

Staffing is the next critical decision. You're not just hiring technical talent — you're hiring stewards of your legacy. Look for professionals who blend financial acumen with discretion, loyalty, and a service mentality. A family office is about trust as much as it is about talent. You'll want a Chief Investment Officer who can coordinate with external managers and build direct investments. A tax strategist who understands not just income tax, but estate, gift, and generation-skipping transfer planning. An estate planning attorney who crafts structures that endure decades. And leadership — typically a CEO or Managing Director — who can align the team around your vision.

Technology also matters. Modern family offices leverage sophisticated reporting systems that integrate investment performance, tax exposure, liquidity needs, and estate planning vehicles into a unified dashboard. Transparency isn't a luxury — it's a requirement. You should be able to see your family's entire financial universe at a glance and drill down as needed.

But structure and staffing are just the mechanics. Culture is the soul of a great family office. Is the focus purely financial, or does it embrace family education, philanthropy, and governance? Does it teach heirs stewardship, or just deliver quarterly reports? Does it create forums for generational dialogue, shared purpose, and values alignment? The best family offices do not merely preserve wealth — they preserve family cohesion.

Pros of establishing a family office include unparalleled control, coordination, and customization. You set the agenda. You define the investment philosophy. You create a tailored legacy strategy. Cons include cost — a robust family office can easily cost 0.25% to 1% of assets under management — and management complexity. It's another enterprise to lead, requiring clear objectives and steady oversight.

Action step: If you feel you're approaching the threshold where complexity is outstripping coordination, begin with a feasibility study. Engage a consultant who specializes in family office setups to audit your current advisory structure, estimate costs, and model potential benefits. It's a small investment that can save enormous headaches — and millions of dollars — down the road.

Because ultimately, setting up a family office is not about opulence. It's about optimization. It's about aligning wealth with values, structure with purpose, generations with a shared mission. It's about turning success into stewardship.

If you're at that point in your journey, don't delay. Build the infrastructure today that will protect, grow, and deploy your wealth intentionally tomorrow. A well-constructed family office is not just a service provider. It's a legacy multiplier.

Chapter 46: Philanthropy, Donating Stock for Maximum Impact

For many ultra-high-net-worth individuals, wealth isn't just a measure of success — it's a tool for significance. At some point, the conversation shifts from how much you have to what you'll do with it. And when you hold significant concentrated stock, philanthropy can become not just an act of generosity but a highly strategic financial move — if executed thoughtfully.

Imagine this: a founder holds $50 million in highly appreciated stock. If sold outright, the tax bill alone could erase tens of millions in value. But if those same shares are donated to a qualified charitable organization — or better yet, to a donor-advised fund or a private foundation — the founder sidesteps capital gains tax, realizes a charitable deduction, and begins deploying that wealth into causes they care about most. It's generosity fused with efficiency — and it's one of the smartest tools in the unwinding playbook.

Donating stock is powerful because it leverages both the asset's appreciation and the current tax code. Rather than selling, paying tax, and then donating what's left, you transfer the shares directly. The charity receives the full value; you get the full deduction (up to 30% of adjusted gross income for appreciated securities), and you avoid the capital gains tax completely. This isn't just theoretical — it's strategy in motion, and one that can amplify both your impact and your after-tax wealth.

But it's not without nuance. Timing matters. If you've held the stock for less than a year, the donation is limited to your cost basis, not the fair market value. Post-IPO lockup periods, insider trading restrictions, and 10b5-1 plans can also affect the transfer. Structuring the donation well before a liquidity event — when the valuation is clear but not yet publicly inflated — can optimize both deduction limits and philanthropic outcomes.

Consider the case of an early tech executive who earmarked a portion of her pre-IPO stock for a donor-advised fund (DAF). By transferring before the IPO, she locked in the fair market value without triggering capital gains, created a reservoir for ongoing charitable giving, and positioned herself for a significant deduction over multiple years. It allowed her to fund scholarships, arts organizations, and medical research — all with the strategic efficiency of a single, well-timed move.

Private foundations offer another route, especially for those who want more control, greater visibility, or a platform for multi-generational giving. But with foundations come increased regulatory scrutiny, administrative costs, and a required minimum distribution of 5% annually. For some, the simplicity and flexibility of a DAF are more attractive. For others, the legacy and permanence of a private foundation are worth the trade-offs. The key is aligning the tool with your goals.

Philanthropy isn't just about the tax benefit. Done well, it can be a unifying force within a family, a vehicle for teaching younger generations about values and stewardship, and a way to stay connected to purpose after a liquidity event. It can also humanize wealth, making it about what you create rather than just what you accumulate. But sloppy execution can undermine these benefits — a rushed or poorly timed donation can mean less impact, lower deductions, or even adverse tax consequences.

Strategic action step: if you're considering charitable giving as part of your concentration unwinding, start early. Engage with your CPA and estate attorney to design a giving strategy that integrates with your broader liquidity and estate plan. Decide whether a DAF, private foundation, or direct giving approach makes the most sense. Think not just about who you'll give to, but how and when to give for maximum effect.

The beauty of philanthropic planning is that it reframes the conversation.

It's no longer just about avoiding taxes or unwinding risk — it's about creating a legacy of impact, about aligning wealth with meaning. And in doing so, you not only preserve capital, but you amplify purpose.

Because ultimately, unwinding concentrated stock isn't just a financial strategy. It's a life strategy. Philanthropy, when approached with care and precision, transforms the concentrated wealth you've built into a diversified legacy of hope, opportunity, and change — a return on investment not measured in dollars, but in lives touched.

Now is the time to think bigger than balance sheets. The next move isn't just about optimizing returns — it's about maximizing impact.

Chapter 47: Avoiding Lifestyle Inflation After a Liquidity Event

It's a scene that plays out more often than many realize. A founder executes a monumental liquidity event—an IPO, a strategic sale, or a secondary offering. Overnight, the balance sheet transforms, and what was once ambition and deferred gratification suddenly becomes actual dollars. The first impulse? Reward. A bigger home. A faster car. Maybe a private jet. After years of relentless work and sacrifice, it feels earned. Deserved, even. But herein lies the trap: lifestyle inflation — the silent tax on success — and if left unchecked, it can quietly undermine even the largest windfalls.

Lifestyle inflation is subtle because it rarely feels like recklessness. You don't wake up and spend half your liquidity on yachts and racehorses. Instead, you make incremental upgrades. You tell yourself the beach house is an investment. The fifth car is just a hobby. The upgraded jet membership is networking. Each decision feels justified — and, to some extent, it is. The problem isn't the individual choices; it's the aggregation. Over time, a higher cost of living becomes the new normal, and what once felt like a cushion starts to feel like a constraint.

The deeper risk is not just financial—it's psychological. Lifestyle inflation shifts the benchmark of satisfaction. When you normalize excess, it dulls the original joy and replaces it with a need for more. What was once a celebration becomes a baseline, and maintaining that baseline requires more liquidity, more risk, and often, more stress. It can quietly erode the freedom that wealth was meant to secure.

Consider a tech founder who sold his company for $150 million. Post-exit, he upgraded his life: a $30 million home, a $5 million car collection, and a personal staff to run it all. Within a few years, what should have been a multi-generational fortune was strained. Not because of bad investments—but because of relentless, creeping lifestyle overhead. When a downturn hit, liquidity dried up, and maintaining that lifestyle became a source of anxiety rather than pride. The dream became a burden.

Now, contrast that with another founder who, after her liquidity event, set clear lifestyle boundaries. She upgraded, but intentionally: one primary residence, thoughtful travel, deliberate generosity. She treated her newfound wealth as a reservoir to create experiences, not just acquire things. As a result, her financial freedom wasn't eroded by lifestyle creep — it was amplified by it. Her wealth served her life, not the other way around.

Avoiding lifestyle inflation isn't about austerity. It's about intentionality. It's about setting an anchor — a personal benchmark for what's "enough." Before the liquidity event even closes, the most disciplined founders and executives map out a "post-liquidity budget." Not a restrictive one, but a thoughtful one. One that allocates for celebration, but also for longevity. For joy, but also for meaning. It's a framework that acknowledges the emotional impulse to spend — and then tempers it with strategy.

A smart action step is to pre-commit to how much of the liquidity event will be carved out for lifestyle upgrades. Maybe it's 5%, maybe 10% — but it's capped. Everything else is earmarked for long-term capital preservation, philanthropy, or entrepreneurial reinvestment. Think of it as "paying yourself a dividend" from the exit — not handing yourself the whole principal.

The benefit of this approach is profound. It preserves optionality. It ensures that even if markets shift, deals sour, or life throws a curveball, the foundation of your wealth remains solid. More importantly, it protects your most valuable asset: freedom. Because true wealth isn't measured by the number of homes or planes you can buy — it's measured by how little you're enslaved to maintaining them.

Philosophically, keeping lifestyle inflation in check is an exercise in stewardship. It recognizes that wealth, once earned, is not just to be spent — it's to be protected, grown, and used to amplify what matters most. Family. Purpose. Legacy. These aren't protected by another villa or another car. They're protected by discipline and clarity.

As you think about unwinding your concentrated stock and preparing for liquidity, don't just plan for the technical aspects—plan for the emotional ones too. Set your lifestyle parameters early. Anchor to values, not just to valuations. Decide what "enough" looks like for you, not based on what others are doing, but based on the life you want to live.

Because in the end, the real risk isn't in selling your stock too quickly or too slowly. It's in squandering the freedom you've worked so hard to build.

Chapter 48: Investing Beyond Stocks, Real Estate, Private Equity, Alternatives

When you've spent years watching your concentrated stock holdings climb, it's natural to think in terms of public equities. Stocks, after all, were how you built your initial wealth. But real wealth management, especially post-liquidity, demands a broader lens. The public markets—while valuable—are just one corner of the investable universe. If you want to truly steward your wealth for decades and generations, you'll need to venture beyond stocks into real estate, private equity, and alternative investments.

Let's start with real estate. For many UHNW individuals, real estate serves a dual purpose: it's both an investment and a tangible asset. Unlike stocks, real estate can generate predictable income streams while offering a hedge against inflation. But it's not without complexity. Direct real estate ownership demands operational expertise—property management, tenant issues, maintenance. For this reason, many choose to access real estate through private real estate funds or REITs (Real Estate Investment Trusts), which offer exposure without the headaches of direct management.

Private equity, on the other hand, taps into a different advantage: access to growth that's often not available in public markets. Founders, by nature, understand this world better than most. After all, you built a company before it was public—or maybe it never even went public. Investing in other private companies, whether through venture capital, growth equity, or buyout funds, leverages your entrepreneurial expertise. But it requires a disciplined approach. Illiquidity is a reality. The capital lock-up can span 7–10 years, and not every investment will hit. Building a diversified private equity allocation—across managers, vintages, and strategies—is key to avoiding concentration risks here as well.

Then there's the broader world of alternative investments: hedge funds, private credit, infrastructure, timber, even art and collectibles. Each offers its own risk-reward profile and, when properly structured, can add valuable diversification. Hedge funds, for example, may employ strategies that aren't dependent on market direction—such as long/short equity or event-driven arbitrage. Private credit funds allow you to act as the lender rather than the borrower, often with higher yields compared to public bonds. But not all alternatives are created equal. Due diligence is critical, as fees can be high and transparency can be limited.

A founder I once advised exited his company and immediately wanted to "get back in the game" by investing heavily in venture capital. The temptation to lean into what you know is powerful—but it can also lead to overexposure. Instead, we developed a framework: a portfolio that included a core allocation to liquid, low-cost public equities and bonds for stability, surrounded by satellites of real estate, private equity, and alternatives. His venture investments were capped at a set percentage of his net worth to maintain balance and avoid emotional decision-making.

Liquidity planning becomes even more important as you diversify. Real estate, private equity, and many alternatives are illiquid. That's part of their appeal—but it also means you must have sufficient liquid assets elsewhere. Think of it as a barbell approach: a portion of your portfolio is highly liquid and accessible; another portion is locked up in long-term, higher-potential strategies. Balancing liquidity with yield and growth potential is how you create a durable portfolio that can withstand market cycles.

Tax considerations also shift as you move beyond public stocks. Private equity funds, for instance, often generate complex K-1 forms with unrelated business taxable income (UBTI) considerations for retirement accounts. Real estate investments can create depreciation benefits, but they can also complicate your tax picture. Working closely with your CPA and wealth advisor to structure investments tax-efficiently is not just smart—it's essential to preserving returns.

Another factor: operational complexity. Managing a portfolio that spans public markets, private investments, real estate, and alternatives requires infrastructure—systems to track performance, manage cash flows, and monitor risk exposures. This is where a family office or outsourced CIO (Chief Investment Officer) model can add immense value. You're not just investing anymore; you're running a sophisticated, multi-asset portfolio.

The goal isn't to replace public equities—it's to complement them. Public markets offer liquidity, transparency, and efficiency. But real estate, private equity, and alternatives add resilience, income, and the potential for outsized returns uncorrelated to stock market volatility. A portfolio built thoughtfully across these domains transforms your wealth from merely accumulated to truly fortified.

As you unwind your concentrated stock positions, remember: wealth is not just about what you earned—it's about what you keep and how you grow it. Investing beyond stocks isn't about chasing returns. It's about building a comprehensive, resilient financial structure that supports not just your lifestyle, but your legacy.

Before you rush to allocate capital, take the time to map your broader goals. Then, assemble a team who can help you execute across multiple asset classes with discipline and clarity. Because the real win isn't owning the next big thing—it's owning the future you envision, with the freedom and flexibility to live it fully.

Chapter 49: Designing Your Legacy, What You Want to Be Remembered For

At some point, every founder, every builder of wealth, reaches a moment when the drive to accumulate transforms into something deeper. It's no longer just about the numbers, the valuations, or the trophies. It's about what those achievements mean—about the mark you'll leave behind. You didn't pour your energy, your intellect, and your time into building a company just to walk away and disappear. The question becomes: What do you want to be remembered for?

Legacy, in the true sense, isn't about monuments or headlines. It's about impact. It's about shaping the lives of the people you care about and the communities you touch. And like everything else you've done well, legacy doesn't happen by accident. It's designed—deliberately, thoughtfully, with intention.

Many founders initially view legacy through the lens of inheritance. How much will I leave to my children? But wealth, left without structure or guidance, can be as much a burden as a gift. Studies have shown that generational wealth often dissipates by the third generation. Not because the fortune wasn't large enough, but because the family wasn't prepared for it. True legacy design requires more than writing a will—it demands instilling values, setting expectations, and equipping the next generation with the tools to steward what you've built.

One founder I worked with created not just a trust, but a family governance structure—a family mission statement, regular meetings, even a "next generation" leadership council for his grandchildren. His legacy wasn't just the wealth he passed down—it was the culture of responsibility, entrepreneurship, and philanthropy he embedded into his family. His money became a platform for opportunity, not entitlement.

Outside the family, legacy extends to the causes you care about. Philanthropy is often thought of as the final act, but for many founders, it's integrated into their life's work. Whether through donor-advised funds, private foundations, or strategic direct giving, thoughtful philanthropy can multiply the impact of your wealth exponentially. But again—design matters. Clear goals, defined missions, and measurable outcomes distinguish effective philanthropy from scattered charity.

Your legacy is also carried forward in the businesses you back, the leaders you mentor, the communities you nurture. Think about how you want to use your expertise, not just your capital, to influence the next generation of builders. Some founders set up family offices that invest directly in startups aligned with their values. Others establish scholarship funds, mentorship programs, or entrepreneurship hubs in underserved areas. Legacy doesn't have to be about scale—it's about resonance.

It's also important to confront the uncomfortable parts of legacy planning. What happens if heirs are not ready or capable? What if visions diverge over time? Building flexibility into your estate plan and governance documents—clear succession plans, trustee structures, and contingency options—can safeguard your legacy from erosion or conflict.

And don't underestimate the emotional legacy you leave. Wealth is one part of what you pass on. But the memories you create, the stories you tell, the values you embody—those are the things that endure in the hearts of those who follow you. Start those conversations now. Share your journey, your struggles, your principles. Help your heirs understand not just what you built, but why.

Designing your legacy means shifting your focus from success to significance. It's a natural evolution for someone who has already achieved what many only dream about. But it requires intentionality. It's not about replicating what others have done. It's about reflecting deeply on what matters most to you—and then crafting a plan to ensure that, long after you're gone, those values continue to shape the world.

As you unwind your concentrated stock, think of it not just as a liquidity event, but as a legacy event. It's the fuel that will power the next phase of your impact. And like any powerful resource, it requires a strategy to be used wisely.

Before the next big investment, the next acquisition, or the next project, take the time to ask yourself: What do I want to be remembered for? And then, start building it. Because wealth fades, businesses evolve, and markets shift—but a well-designed legacy endures.

Chapter 50: The Final Move, From Concentrated Founder to Wise Steward of Wealth

For years, your identity was wrapped in your company—the late nights, the impossible problems, the thrill of winning deals and building something from scratch. You didn't just build a business; you built value, impact, and wealth. But at some point, the equation changes. When you're sitting on a mountain of concentrated stock, the challenge is no longer how to build it higher. The real challenge becomes how to protect it, preserve it, and deploy it wisely. It's the pivot from founder to steward, and it's a transition that deserves the same care and strategy you gave your company.

Many founders wrestle with this shift. After all, building is dynamic, aggressive, risk-seeking. Stewardship, by contrast, can feel unfamiliar—patient, measured, disciplined. But make no mistake: true stewardship is every bit as complex and demanding as entrepreneurship. It requires strategic thinking, rigorous planning, and a steady hand. The difference is that now, the stakes aren't just your own—they're generational.

Becoming a wise steward of wealth begins with letting go of old mindsets. Concentrated wealth is exhilarating because it offers the allure of outsized gains. But it's also perilous because it exposes you to outsized risk. Stewardship demands a new lens: seeing risk not as something to conquer but as something to manage thoughtfully. It's about preserving your wealth against the inevitable storms—market volatility, tax law changes, inflation, unforeseen crises—without surrendering its potential to grow.

The first move for many founders is tactical: a liquidity event, a sale, a transfer. But the real first move is mental. It's the decision to shift from accumulation to preservation and purpose. It's no longer about maximizing returns at all costs. It's about maximizing resilience, sustainability, and impact. That begins with diversification—intentionally unwinding concentrated positions and redeploying assets into a broader, more durable portfolio.

Stewardship also demands structure. You didn't build your company without an organizational chart, a set of systems, a clear mission. Your wealth deserves the same. Whether through a family office, a carefully curated team of advisors, or a mix of trusts, investment vehicles, and philanthropic entities, wise stewardship is built on infrastructure that clarifies decision-making and ensures alignment with your values and goals.

Another hallmark of the wise steward is a long-term perspective. When you're in founder mode, you're often measured in quarterly results and five-year exit plans. As a steward, the horizon stretches further—across decades, even generations. That means thinking beyond investment performance to governance, succession planning, and the cultivation of the next generation of stewards in your family.

One founder I advised made this pivot with remarkable clarity. After the sale of his company, he didn't rush to deploy capital. He spent a year educating himself, designing a governance structure for his family's new wealth, and building an investment policy that balanced growth with preservation. He treated his family capital like an enduring enterprise, not a windfall. Today, his family council meets quarterly, and his wealth is invested across public markets, private equity, real estate, and impact ventures—all mapped carefully to a 50-year vision.

Of course, stewardship isn't just about the numbers. It's about what the numbers make possible. Philanthropy, impact investing, mentorship—these become not side projects but central chapters in the story you're writing with your wealth. Stewardship asks not just "How much can I leave behind?" but "How will what I leave behind shape the world after me?"

The transition from founder to steward is not a downgrade—it's an evolution. It's a move from the adrenaline of the sprint to the wisdom of the marathon. It's recognizing that the goal is not just to build wealth but to make it work—to make it endure, inspire, and empower.

As you stand at this inflection point, the question isn't whether you can succeed. You've already proven that. The real question is whether you can channel the same discipline, vision, and passion that built your fortune into stewarding it wisely. If you do, you won't just be remembered as a builder of companies. You'll be remembered as a builder of legacies.

And that, ultimately, is the final move worth mastering.

Important Disclaimer

Important Information About Unwinding Concentrated Stock

Unwinding Concentrated Stock is written to educate, empower, and encourage successful founders, executives, and families with significant concentrated wealth to take control of their financial lives, liquidity planning, and long-term legacy building. The insights in this book are based on the author's personal experience, professional training, and more than two decades of work in financial services, private wealth management, and advising high-net-worth and ultra-high-net-worth clients.

That said, it's important to be clear about what this book is — and what it is not.

Educational Purpose Only

All content in *Unwinding Concentrated Stock* is provided for general educational and informational purposes only. It is intended to introduce accomplished individuals and families to essential principles of managing concentrated stock risk, liquidity event planning, strategic diversification, and multi-generational wealth stewardship.

While this book shares frameworks, strategies, case studies, and real-world examples, it is not personalized financial advice. Every individual's circumstances are unique. Your stock holdings, liquidity timeline, tax situation, risk appetite, estate planning needs, and family dynamics must all be carefully considered.

Before making significant financial, legal, tax, or business decisions, you should work with licensed professionals who understand your specific circumstances and goals.

No Legal Advice

Although managing concentrated stock often intersects with estate planning, trust structures, corporate law, and charitable giving, this book does not provide legal advice. It is not a substitute for consulting a qualified attorney.

If you are:

- Drafting or updating trusts, wills, or estate plans
- Structuring or dissolving family partnerships or corporate entities
- Managing liquidity events across multiple jurisdictions
- Planning charitable giving through foundations or donor-advised funds
- Setting up asset protection strategies

...you should seek the expertise of an experienced attorney who specializes in estate, business, and philanthropic planning. Laws and regulations vary, and personalized legal advice is critical for your protection and success.

No Financial or Investment Advice

This book discusses important topics such as unwinding stock concentration, asset allocation, liquidity strategies, risk mitigation, wealth transfer, and long-term investing — but strictly from an educational perspective.

Unwinding Concentrated Stock is not written by a Certified Financial Planner™, Registered Investment Advisor, or broker-dealer. The strategies and examples presented are general in nature and may not directly apply to your specific situation.

Before implementing any investment strategies, reallocating your holdings, or executing a diversification plan, consult a qualified financial advisor or wealth manager with expertise in concentrated wealth and liquidity event planning.

No Accounting or Tax Advice

Tax optimization is a vital component of unwinding concentrated wealth, but this book is not written by a CPA, Enrolled Agent, or licensed tax professional. Any discussion around tax efficiency, capital gains management, gifting strategies, or estate tax minimization is for general educational purposes only.

If you are:

- Structuring trusts or family entities
- Navigating capital gains and AMT considerations
- Leveraging Section 1202 (QSBS) benefits
- Planning for liquidity events, business exits, or succession
- Designing charitable giving strategies to enhance tax outcomes

...you should engage a tax advisor who specializes in high-net-worth and ultra-high-net-worth planning. Only a qualified tax professional can deliver advice tailored to your unique situation and ensure compliance with current tax laws.

No Guarantees or Promises

Reading this book does not guarantee financial success, risk elimination, tax savings, or preservation of wealth. Effective wealth management and strategic planning require thoughtful action, collaboration with professionals, and the ability to adapt to changing circumstances.

The case studies and scenarios presented are illustrative and for educational purposes only. They are not forecasts of future performance or guarantees of success. Your financial results will depend on a wide range of factors, including your decisions, market conditions, legislative changes, and unforeseen life events.

Limitation of Liability

By reading this book, you agree that the author, Pat Brown, MBA, and any affiliated brands — including FinancialLiteracyForNIL.com and related platforms — are not responsible for your financial outcomes, legal matters, tax liabilities, or investment results.

Neither the author nor any associated entity shall be held liable for any losses, penalties, or negative outcomes resulting from your use of the information in this book. You are fully responsible for your financial, legal, and investment decisions.

Encouragement to Build Your Professional Team

The author firmly believes that individuals and families managing concentrated wealth need a coordinated team of advisors:

- A financial advisor or wealth manager
- A tax professional (CPA or international tax specialist)
- An estate planning attorney
- A business attorney
- An insurance consultant
- A philanthropic advisor

This book is designed to complement — not replace — the expertise of your advisory team. If you have not yet built a team of experienced professionals around you, now is the time. Managing concentrated wealth and executing a thoughtful liquidity strategy demands careful coordination and expertise.

You've invested years, perhaps decades, creating extraordinary value and wealth. Now it's time to protect, preserve, and extend that success — for yourself, for your family, and for the impact you want to have on the world.

Managing Concentrated Wealth: Orchestrating a Legacy Beyond a Single Stock

At the ultra-affluent level, managing wealth—especially concentrated stock wealth—is not a singular endeavor. It is a complex, interconnected system that demands more than casual attention; it requires mastery. Successfully unwinding a concentrated stock position and preserving wealth for generations is not about one smart move or one good year. It is about orchestrating a strategic framework where estate planning, tax optimization, insurance protection, investment management, trading, liquidity planning, and philanthropy work in concert. Done right, this orchestration transforms complexity into clarity, risk into resilience, and concentrated wealth into a living legacy.

Estate planning is non-negotiable. Concentrated stock, particularly with a low-cost basis, carries significant estate implications if left unchecked. Properly coordinated trusts—GRATs, dynasty trusts, and family partnerships—can not only mitigate estate taxes but ensure that wealth passes seamlessly and efficiently to future generations. Real-life scenario: A founder with a $100 million single-stock position transferred shares into a series of grantor retained annuity trusts, significantly reducing his taxable estate while maintaining control and setting up future generations for success. Action Step: Revisit your estate plan to ensure it is robust, tax-optimized, and actively working to transition your concentrated wealth according to your legacy goals.

Tax planning must be dynamic and preemptive. Concentrated stock positions create significant tax risks—capital gains exposure, AMT triggers, and liquidity event taxation. Sophisticated planning between your wealth manager, CPA, and tax attorney ensures you can unwind with minimal friction. Techniques like tax-loss harvesting, QSBS exemptions, gifting strategies, and domicile optimization must be part of the dialogue early and often. Pros: Lower tax bills and higher net retention of wealth. Cons: Requires coordination and constant attention to shifting regulations. Action Step: Assemble a tax team with experience navigating the complexity of large, concentrated positions and mandate regular strategy sessions.

Insurance planning is your silent safeguard. Many affluent individuals underestimate the risks that can accompany significant concentrated wealth. Concentrated positions may invite litigation risk, complicate succession planning, or exacerbate estate issues. Properly structured umbrella policies, life insurance trusts, and asset protection plans are essential. Real-life scenario: A founder was advised to structure a large life insurance policy inside an ILIT (irrevocable life insurance trust), providing estate liquidity without adding to the taxable estate. Action Step: Perform a risk audit that includes all facets of your wealth—personal, corporate, and philanthropic—and align insurance strategies accordingly.

Investment management must transition from concentration to customization. Your concentrated stock has served you well, but the future demands a diversified strategy aligned with your risk tolerance, liquidity needs, and legacy aspirations. Direct indexing, private equity, venture capital, real estate, and alternative strategies should replace concentrated risk with a diversified, tax-efficient portfolio. Action Step: Build an investment policy statement that reflects not only your goals but your new reality—one where no single company's fortunes determine your family's future.

Trading and execution take on heightened importance when unwinding large blocks of stock. Block sales, 10b5-1 plans, and sophisticated trading desks minimize market impact and preserve value. Tax-loss harvesting opportunities can be maximized when paired with disciplined selling strategies. Real-life scenario: A family office systematically sold down a large public stock position via a 10b5-1 plan, avoiding abrupt market moves and optimizing capital gains taxes. Action Step: Partner with a trading desk that specializes in handling large, complex positions discreetly and tax-efficiently.

Liquidity and exit planning must begin long before a liquidity event. Whether you're approaching an IPO lock-up expiration, contemplating a secondary market sale, or planning a strategic business exit, liquidity should be seen not just as cashing out, but as redeploying capital intentionally. Real-life scenario: A founder pre-funded charitable vehicles and dynasty trusts ahead of a liquidity event, locking in tax advantages and spreading out risk. Action Step: If liquidity is anywhere on your horizon, begin coordinating estate, tax, and investment strategies today—not when the check clears.

Philanthropy should be integrated, not isolated. Concentrated wealth can fuel tremendous impact when aligned with strategic giving vehicles like donor-advised funds, private foundations, or charitable remainder trusts. Done thoughtfully, giving back can also be an effective tool for reducing estate and capital gains taxes while engaging the next generation in shared family values. Action Step: Create a philanthropy strategy that sits alongside your broader wealth plan, reinforcing both impact and efficiency.

The complexity across all these areas is dynamic. Markets shift. Tax laws evolve. Family needs change. Your concentrated stock position should be the beginning of your strategy—not the centerpiece of your future. Effective coordination across estate planning, tax strategy, investment management, risk protection, and philanthropy turns a once-volatile position into a structured, resilient legacy. Real-life scenario: A multi-generational family office integrated liquidity planning, estate structures, philanthropy, and investment diversification—turning concentrated success into generational security. Action Step: Assemble a team capable of true coordination, not just isolated excellence.

The message is simple: complexity requires orchestration. Managing concentrated wealth is not about isolated brilliance in one domain—it is about integrated mastery across all domains. Your goals—preservation, growth, tax efficiency, family unity, and legacy building—are attainable. But only with a deliberate, harmonized approach.

While *Unwinding Concentrated Stock* is designed to be an educational guide, if you find yourself needing deeper, tailored advice on executing this level of strategic coordination, Pat Brown would be honored to help. With years of experience advising ultra-affluent families and a passion for navigating complexity with precision and discretion, Pat is committed to helping you transform your concentrated wealth into an enduring legacy.

Financial Literacy Is Powerful — But Only If You Act on It

Financial Literacy Is Powerful — But Only If You Act on It

Knowledge alone doesn't change your financial future. Action does. Especially at the ultra-affluent level, financial literacy must translate into deliberate, strategic moves if you want to transform concentrated stock into sustainable wealth and lasting legacy.

Here's a strategic checklist designed to help ultra-affluent individuals and families move beyond understanding — and into powerful execution.

Start with a full audit of your personal and family finances. True clarity begins with a detailed review of personal cash flow, savings, and liquidity reserves. Assess your family office or private entity structures — are they operating with maximum efficiency and flexibility? Know your personal runway — how long can you maintain your lifestyle without disruptive changes? And perhaps more importantly, know the family's collective runway. In a world where liquidity and agility are non-negotiable, understanding your capital position is foundational.

Next, evaluate your business and private holdings. Concentrated wealth often extends beyond public stock positions into ownership stakes in operating businesses, private equity, and venture capital. Understand where you are on the liquidity timeline for these investments. When are key valuations due? Are exit strategies clearly outlined? Confirm that your governance structures — including shareholder agreements, buy-sell arrangements, and management succession plans — are not just legally current but strategically aligned with your long-term vision.

Strengthen your liquidity and emergency planning. In times of uncertainty or opportunity, liquidity is your greatest asset. Ensure you have ready access to cash equivalents covering 12 to 24 months of personal and family obligations. Secure standby credit facilities or alternative liquidity lines to cover unexpected capital needs. Waiting until you "need" liquidity often means accepting suboptimal terms. Advance preparation puts you in control.

Maximize your tax-advantaged structures and retirement planning. Ultra-affluent individuals can access powerful tools like defined benefit plans, deferred compensation arrangements, and private placement life insurance (PPLI) — structures designed to optimize tax efficiency and wealth transfer. 529 plans for education funding, donor-advised funds (DAFs) for philanthropy, and grantor trusts for strategic gifting should also be part of the conversation. Every dollar preserved from taxation is another dollar preserved for your family or mission.

Protect yourself, your family, and your legacy. Risk management isn't glamorous, but it's essential. Audit personal insurance policies — life, disability, umbrella, cyber, and liability — and ensure they reflect the current value of your assets and lifestyle. Don't stop there: review business insurance coverage like key person, directors and officers (D&O), and corporate liability policies. Update intellectual property protections and ensure that asset ownership structures — including trusts, partnerships, and LLCs — are properly designed to shield and preserve wealth.

Plan for taxes early and strategically. Taxes are not just a year-end discussion — they should be embedded into every financial decision you make. Engage a tax team skilled in managing complex portfolios, business holdings, and multi-jurisdictional assets. Start preparing for liquidity events years in advance, not months. Explore opportunities under the Qualified Small Business Stock (QSBS) exemption, 1031 like-kind exchanges for real estate, and sophisticated trust strategies to minimize capital gains, estate, and income tax exposures.

Establish or update your estate plan. The structures that once made sense may no longer serve your current goals or tax landscape. Create or revise foundational documents — wills, revocable and irrevocable trusts, durable powers of attorney. Consider dynasty trusts, GRATs, SLATs, or charitable remainder trusts to better steward your concentrated wealth for generations. Legacy planning is not just legal paperwork — it's the architecture of how your life's work carries forward. Family governance and succession planning should be woven into the strategy early and often.

Diversify beyond core holdings. Concentration creates wealth; diversification preserves it. Resist the inertia of familiarity. No matter how attached you are to a single company, asset class, or sector, true security comes from building a globally diversified portfolio aligned with your long-term goals and personal risk tolerance. Real estate, private equity, hedge funds, fixed income, and global equities — consider all parts of the investable universe, thoughtfully and strategically.

Build and maintain your professional advisory team. Your wealth demands expertise at every level. Ensure you have a CPA familiar with multi-entity, multi-jurisdictional structures; a financial advisor experienced with ultra-affluent families and family offices; an estate attorney skilled in advanced trust planning and family governance; and an insurance consultant who can customize protection for complex lives. Surround yourself with seasoned professionals who collaborate, not just operate in silos.

Set quarterly financial strategy reviews. Wealth management is dynamic. Family circumstances, tax laws, markets, and even your personal aspirations evolve. Schedule quarterly strategy sessions to review progress and adjust course. Monitor wealth transfer plans, investment performance, tax positioning, and your family's evolving goals. Success at the ultra-affluent level is built on iteration, not complacency.

Final Reminder:

Start where you are. You don't have to master every topic overnight. Financial literacy at this level isn't about chasing perfection — it's about sustained, intentional action. Small, disciplined moves, compounded over time, produce extraordinary outcomes. Strategic action aligned with your wealth, values, and legacy transforms concentrated stock into an enduring foundation for generations.

Professional Wealth Management: Why DIY Is Rarely Enough at the Ultra-Affluent Level

When it comes to unwinding concentrated stock and managing significant wealth, the inevitable question arises: Should you manage it yourself, or engage a professional team? For the ultra-affluent, this decision is far too consequential to be left to intuition or convenience. The complexity of concentrated assets, tax law intricacies, risk exposures, liquidity planning, and long-term legacy aspirations turn wealth management from a personal endeavor into a professional discipline. At this level, the allure of self-management appeals to the independent spirit, but the realities of strategy and scale often make professional orchestration indispensable.

Time is the first hidden cost of DIY wealth management. Unwinding a concentrated stock position and overseeing an ultra-high-net-worth (UHNW) portfolio demand relentless attention to shifting tax laws, market dynamics, estate structures, liquidity strategies, and family governance. Attempting to manage this complexity personally comes at a steep opportunity cost — time diverted from building the next venture, nurturing family, or pursuing passions. Action Step: Conduct an honest audit of the time required to manage your wealth in its entirety and weigh it against the time you want to reclaim for your life and legacy.

The challenge compounds with complexity. Managing multiple legal entities, layered trusts, offshore holdings, private equity stakes, operating companies, and philanthropic vehicles requires specialized knowledge and coordinated strategy. Real-Life Scenario: A tech entrepreneur who sold his business for $500 million tried to manage post-sale planning independently but quickly found the intricate tax filings across five jurisdictions overwhelming, eventually assembling a professional team within two years. Action Step: Map the complexity of your holdings and benchmark what a fully professionalized structure would look like.

Emotional distance is a profound yet often overlooked advantage of professional management. When you've built the business, selected the investments, and nurtured the assets, emotional bias is inevitable. A seasoned wealth manager provides a critical layer of objectivity, making decisions based on disciplined strategy rather than personal attachment. Pros: Clear-eyed advice and reduced cognitive bias. Cons: Potential loss of direct control if not structured with collaboration in mind. Action Step: Evaluate where emotional bias may be clouding your judgment and consider how a neutral third party can add strategic clarity.

Access to opportunity widens dramatically with professional management. Some of the most valuable investments — elite venture capital funds, private placements, direct real estate syndicates — are inaccessible to all but the best-connected. A professional manager with institutional relationships can open doors that DIY investors simply cannot. Real-Life Scenario: A professionally managed family office secured an allocation in a highly selective private equity fund that ultimately tripled their capital — an opportunity not available on the open market. Action Step: Evaluate the caliber and exclusivity of opportunities currently available to you and whether your network is truly delivering.

Tax mitigation is not optional — it's central to wealth preservation — but it's also highly technical. Strategies like QSBS exemptions, offshore insurance wrappers, GRATs, and generation-skipping trusts are powerful, but nuanced. Without deep expertise, even the well-read affluent individual risks missed opportunities or costly missteps. Action Step: Commit to a proactive, multi-year tax strategy focused on multi-generational wealth, not just year-to-year savings.

Risk management must be holistic. For the ultra-affluent, market risk is just one dimension. Enterprise risk, reputational risk, cyber risk, legal exposure, and family risk all loom large. Professionals integrate insurance strategies, legal structures, cybersecurity protocols, and portfolio hedges into a cohesive plan. Action Step: Demand a comprehensive risk audit across every layer of your financial and personal life — not just your investments.

Family governance and legacy planning present some of the most delicate, high-stakes challenges. Managing concentrated wealth for a lifetime is one thing; stewarding it across generations is another. Formal governance — educational initiatives, mission statements, family constitutions, and succession frameworks — ensures alignment and stability. Real-Life Scenario: One UHNW family fractured after the patriarch's death without a governance structure in place, while another transitioned seamlessly under professional guidance. Action Step: Establish or refine your family governance strategy with expert facilitation.

Cost is a natural concern when considering professional management, but it must be viewed in context. The true cost is not the fee — it's the missed investment opportunities, tax inefficiencies, legal vulnerabilities, and disjointed strategies that erode wealth over time. Pros: Expertise, risk mitigation, coordinated strategy. Cons: Management fees, which are justifiable if your team delivers exponential value. Action Step: Evaluate the net benefit of professional management in terms of enhanced returns, risk reduction, and strategic clarity.

The decision between DIY and professional wealth management is not binary. Many ultra-affluent individuals adopt a hybrid model — retaining involvement in high-level strategy while entrusting execution and day-to-day oversight to trusted professionals. The key lies in recognizing that wealth at this scale demands orchestration, expertise, and emotional discipline that few individuals can sustain alone.

The call to action is clear: Don't just ask if you *can* manage your wealth alone — ask if you *should*. Concentrated wealth is not merely an asset to protect; it's a responsibility to manage with wisdom, rigor, and vision. Preservation, strategic growth, risk management, opportunity access, and legacy fulfillment are achievable — but only with the expertise, discipline, and coordination that a professional team delivers.

While this book was designed to empower your understanding, if you recognize the need for deeper, personalized support in unwinding concentrated stock and stewarding wealth, Pat Brown would be honored to be of service. With extensive experience guiding ultra-affluent families and individuals through complexity with precision, Pat offers the discretion, strategic depth, and comprehensive coordination necessary to elevate your wealth — and your legacy — to its fullest potential.

Mastering Your Financial Year: A Strategic Calendar for the Ultra-Affluent

Managing significant wealth—especially when unwinding a concentrated stock position—is not unlike running a sophisticated, multi-generational enterprise. It demands clarity, structure, and adaptability. Success isn't accidental at this level; it's engineered through disciplined cycles of review and adjustment. This month-by-month blueprint is designed to help ultra-affluent individuals and families structure their financial year with precision and intention, ensuring that complexity is managed, not neglected.

JANUARY

January 1 signals a reset of contribution limits for retirement plans—401(k), 403(b), 457 accounts, and IRAs. Health Savings Account (HSA) and Flexible Spending Account (FSA) thresholds also reset. Start the year with a full review of personal, business, and family office budgets. Confirm your liquidity runway is intact and adjust paycheck withholdings if major life events—marriage, divorce, new family additions—occurred last year.

January 15 brings the deadline for Fourth Quarter Estimated Taxes—review closely, especially if liquidity events have shifted your income landscape. Late January is when W-2s, 1099s, and other tax documents start arriving—begin compiling early.

FEBRUARY

By February 1, employers and institutions must issue W-2s and 1099s. Partnership K-1s may begin trickling in later in the month. Now is the time to organize tax documentation for all entities: personal, business, trusts, private investments, and real estate holdings. Strategic tax positioning starts with complete, organized data.

MARCH

March 15 looms large: the tax filing deadline for partnerships and S-corporations. Extensions can be filed, but preparation should not be delayed. March 31 brings deadlines for receiving health coverage forms. If you're managing or unwinding complex structures, use this window to ensure that everything—cash flow models, tax strategies, liquidity projections—remains updated and in sync.

APRIL

April is tax month, and April 15 is the annual filing deadline for individual returns and the first installment of estimated taxes for the year ahead. If you turned 73 last year, April 1 marks the deadline to take your first Required Minimum Distribution (RMD). Max out prior-year contributions to IRAs, HSAs, and SEPs if applicable. This is also FAFSA season for college-bound family members—wealthy families often assume they're ineligible, but strategic positioning matters.

MAY

Early May is a smart time to review property tax assessments; inaccuracies could be costing you significantly. May 29—5/29 Day—is a timely reminder to review 529 college savings plans. Even for the ultra-affluent, strategic tax-advantaged vehicles for education funding remain a cornerstone of multi-generational planning.

JUNE

June 15 marks the Second Quarter Estimated Tax deadline. For U.S. citizens living abroad, it's also the personal tax filing deadline. Mid-year is an ideal time to review portfolios, rebalance allocations, and reassess charitable giving strategies. Unwinding a concentrated position should happen in context—not just with market conditions, but with family goals, tax optimization, and legacy planning in mind.

JULY

July offers a natural mid-year checkpoint. Conduct a full financial check-in: spending, saving, debt progress, and liquidity planning. Review investment allocations in light of current markets and meet with your advisory team—wealth advisors, CPAs, estate attorneys—to ensure alignment across strategies.

AUGUST

Preparation for Open Enrollment begins now. Review healthcare, disability, and life insurance policies. Audit HSA/FSA balances and strategize around year-end charitable giving, appreciated stock donations, and Qualified Charitable Distributions (QCDs). If you are actively unwinding stock positions, August is the time to confirm whether you'll use appreciated assets for philanthropy before year-end deadlines.

SEPTEMBER

September 15 closes the window for Third Quarter Estimated Taxes and extended partnership and S-corp returns. It's a smart time to revisit tax-loss harvesting strategies. Late September is ideal for reviewing Backdoor Roth IRA conversions and confirming any last moves that may reduce your taxable footprint.

OCTOBER

October 1 is the deadline to establish SIMPLE IRAs for the current year, and October 15 marks the extended individual tax return deadline. Open Enrollment periods typically begin this month; review all employer and personal benefits packages closely.

NOVEMBER

The Affordable Care Act (ACA) Marketplace and many employer benefits enrollment windows open in November. It's your final opportunity to optimize retirement plan contributions, health insurance elections, and HSA/FSA funding levels before year-end. Black Friday weekend is also a timely checkpoint: high-ticket purchases should align with broader cash flow and tax planning strategies.

DECEMBER

The last month of the year is critical for tying up loose ends. Ensure maximum contributions to 401(k)s, 403(b)s, and 457 plans. Complete any charitable gifts, tax-loss harvesting, and RMDs if applicable. It's also your final chance to make annual tax-free gifts (currently $18,000 per recipient). If you're managing a family office or private entity, this is bonus season—profit-sharing or discretionary bonuses must be issued before year-end to be deductible.

Rolling & Event-Based Reminders

Throughout the year, synchronize your wealth strategies with key life events—marriages, divorces, births, adoptions, relocations, or liquidity events. Quarterly reviews should include budgeting, investment assessments, and execution of strategic tax moves such as Roth conversions and tax-loss harvesting.

Final Tip: Structure and Automate for Strategic Success

Financial mastery at the ultra-affluent level thrives on discipline. Set automated calendar alerts for major deadlines. Automate contributions to savings and investment vehicles. Pre-schedule quarterly strategy reviews with your advisory team. Pre-plan debt servicing and philanthropic initiatives. The fewer tasks left to chance, the more consistently you will execute against a plan designed not just for growth—but for stewardship and lasting legacy.

Financial literacy is powerful, but disciplined action transforms knowledge into generational wealth.

30 Questions Ultra-Affluent Individuals Should Ask Their Professionals

Questions to Ask a Financial Advisor

1. Are you a fiduciary 100% of the time?
2. Do you have experience working with ultra-affluent families, tech founders, and entrepreneurs with complex equity compensation?
3. How do you get paid—fee-only, fee-based, or commission?
4. Can you help with equity compensation planning, including stock options, RSUs, pre-IPO shares, and liquidity event strategies?
5. Will you coordinate with my CPA, estate attorney, insurance specialist, and other key advisors?
6. What's your investment philosophy, and how do you incorporate private equity, venture capital, and direct deals?
7. How do you help clients prepare for major liquidity events, acquisitions, or IPOs?
8. Can you advise on risk management, including asset protection structures and insurance?
9. Are you familiar with advanced retirement planning for entrepreneurs (e.g., Cash Balance Plans, Defined Benefit Plans)?
10. Do you provide scenario planning and Monte Carlo simulations to stress-test financial strategies?

Questions to Ask a CPA

1. Do you specialize in working with ultra-affluent individuals, en-

trepreneurs, and clients with cross-border or multi-state tax complexities?

2. Do you provide proactive, year-round tax planning instead of only preparing returns?
3. Are you experienced with Qualified Small Business Stock (QSBS) and Section 1202 exclusions?
4. Can you advise on optimizing charitable giving strategies, including Donor-Advised Funds and Private Foundations?
5. How do you handle clients with international holdings, residency considerations, or multi-jurisdictional income?
6. Will you represent me in the event of an IRS audit or tax dispute?
7. Can you consult on real estate investments, 1031 exchanges, and Opportunity Zone strategies?
8. How do you coordinate tax planning with my estate attorney and financial advisor?

Questions to Ask an Estate Planning Attorney

1. Do you have experience working with founders, entrepreneurs, and ultra-high-net-worth families?
2. What core documents should I have in place—wills, revocable living trusts, irrevocable trusts, POAs, healthcare directives?
3. Can you advise on asset protection strategies, including domestic and offshore trusts?
4. How do you handle estate planning for business owners, stock options, and liquidity events?
5. Should I consider advanced structures like GRATs, SLATs, IDGTs, or Dynasty Trusts?
6. Can you help design a family governance framework and succession plan for wealth continuity?
7. How often should I review and update my estate plan given changing tax laws and family dynamics?

Questions to Ask a Business Attorney

1. Do you specialize in startups, venture-backed companies, or scaling tech businesses?
2. Can you advise on entity formation, Delaware incorporation, and ownership structure optimization?
3. Will you review or draft shareholder agreements, IP assignments, employment contracts, and fundraising documents?
4. Can you advise on mergers, acquisitions, and exit strategies, including due diligence preparation?
5. How do you structure your fees—hourly, flat rate, or retainer—and can you provide transparency up front?

Bonus Questions for Other Key Professionals

Insurance Advisor

- Are you independent or affiliated with a carrier (captive agent)?
- Can you tailor a comprehensive insurance portfolio, including personal, business, and estate liquidity needs?
- Should I consider key person insurance or buy-sell agreements for my business?
- How do you balance term life versus permanent life insurance strategies for wealth transfer?

Real Estate Advisor

- Are you experienced with evaluating real estate from an investment and tax optimization perspective?
- Can you guide transactions involving 1031 exchanges or Opportunity Zone investments?

Executive Coach or Career Consultant

- Can you coach on life transitions—founder burnout, post-exit reinvention, or pivoting to venture investing?
- Can you model financial and lifestyle impacts of different career paths or "next chapters" post-liquidity?

Final Thought

Choosing your professional team—financial advisor, CPA, estate attorney, business attorney, insurance consultant, real estate strategist—is one of the highest-leverage decisions you'll ever make. Ask sharp questions. Demand transparent, thoughtful answers. Build a team that matches the scale of your wealth and the ambition of your legacy.

While this guide is for informational purposes, if you require guidance, Pat Brown would be honored to assist—bringing years of experience in advising ultra-affluent individuals through every stage of wealth stewardship and legacy planning.

About The Author

Pat Brown, MBA, is a former Division I football player turned wealth advisor, educator, and nationally respected voice in financial literacy. With more than two decades of experience in financial planning, investment strategy, and insurance, Pat has dedicated his career to helping ultra-affluent individuals, families, and entrepreneurs build wealth with clarity, confidence, and a long-term vision.

After earning his MBA and launching a successful career in wealth management, Pat founded a series of financial literacy platforms designed to serve a wide range of high-achieving, often underserved, communities. His platforms include:

- Financial Literacy For NIL
- Financial Literacy For Student Athletes
- Financial Literacy For The Culture
- Financial Literacy For College Coaches
- Financial Literacy For Parents of Student Athletes
- Financial Literacy For Attorneys
- Financial Literacy For Doctors
- Financial Literacy For Dentists
- Financial Literacy For Pharmacists
- Financial Literacy For Engineers
- Financial Literacy For First Responders
- Financial Literacy For Expats
- Financial Literacy For Architects

Now, through *Ultra Affluent,* Pat brings his mission to the individuals and families managing significant wealth—those who understand that success is not just about accumulation, but stewardship, strategy, and legacy. Ultra-affluent individuals are experts in their professions, industries, and ventures—but even the most accomplished leaders often have not been taught how to apply that same strategic rigor to their personal wealth.

Pat's passion for financial education is deeply personal. Raised in a home where money discussions were scarce, he saw firsthand how the absence of financial literacy could derail even the brightest futures. Today, Pat is committed to bridging the gap between income and enduring wealth—ensuring that success translates into multigenerational security and opportunity.

Over the years, Pat has become a trusted advisor to a diverse and discerning clientele—including entrepreneurs, attorneys, physicians, executives, investors, and high-net-worth families. His approach is practical, culturally aware, and grounded in real-world experience—free from jargon and pretense. Whether you are overseeing a family office, navigating complex business holdings, preparing for a major liquidity event, or planning your family legacy, Pat's guidance is designed to meet you where you are and guide you forward—strategically and thoughtfully.

Beyond his financial work, Pat serves as a Trustee on the Board of Lawrence Memorial Hospital (LMH), contributing to governance and strategic planning initiatives. He is active on multiple nonprofit and civic boards, championing financial literacy, family support services, and improved access to healthcare.

Above all, Pat is a devoted husband and father. When he's not advising clients or speaking at wealth management forums, family office summits, or industry conferences, he translates complex financial concepts into real-world strategies that ultra-affluent individuals and families can immediately apply to secure and elevate their futures.

Pat believes financial literacy at the ultra-affluent level isn't just about wealth—it's about options, freedom, responsibility, and crafting a legacy of purpose and impact. Just as leaders transform bold ideas into world-changing ventures, Pat helps them transform success into significance—and income into enduring wealth.

Final Word

Need Help? Start Here

Unwinding Concentrated Stock exists because financial literacy is one of the most powerful tools an ultra-affluent individual or family can possess. When applied with intention, it opens doors, protects legacies, and equips you to make strategic, confident financial decisions as your wealth evolves.

However, enduring success—whether in business, investments, or personal wealth management—doesn't come from guesswork. It's built on structure, discipline, and strategic clarity. True mastery at this level isn't about handling every technical detail yourself; it's about knowing how to navigate complexity with precision and when to engage trusted experts to help orchestrate the big picture.

Think of this book as your guide—not a rulebook. Let it spark action. Let it build momentum. But remember: it is not a substitute for tailored advice. Stay curious. Stay intentional. Ask the right questions before making significant financial, legal, tax, or business decisions.

Trusted Resources

If you're ready for deeper discussions, more personalized strategy, or tailored advice about concentrated stock management, liquidity planning, or legacy building, reach out to a professional who understands the unique demands of ultra-affluent wealth—cross-border considerations, pre-IPO planning, risk management, multi-generational succession, private investments, and strategic philanthropy.

Pat Brown, MBA

Wealth Advisor | Financial Literacy Advocate | Former Division I Athlete

Advisor to ultra-affluent individuals, entrepreneurs, founders, executives, and family offices nationwide.

- **Website:** www.unwindingconcentratedstock.com
- **Email:** info@unwindingconcentratedstock.com
- **LinkedIn:** linkedin.com/in/patrickbrownmba

Join Our Newsletter

Stay informed with expert insights and strategies designed for individuals and families managing significant concentrated wealth.

Subscribe at www.unwindingconcentratedstock.com to receive actionable education and advanced planning ideas—delivered directly to your inbox.

Final Word: Use This—Don't Shelf It

The frameworks and strategies in *Unwinding Concentrated Stock* are not meant to sit on a shelf. Use them. Revisit them often. Share them with trusted family members, partners, and advisors. Test what fits your situation. Adjust what doesn't. Keep refining your approach.

This book is your playbook—not just for wealth management, but for building a lasting legacy. Personally. Professionally. Generationally.

Stay sharp. Stay curious. Keep shaping the future you deserve.

Questions or Need Additional Help?

Pat Brown welcomes meaningful conversations. For personalized planning, concentrated stock strategy sessions, or guidance tailored to your unique wealth journey, visit www.unwindingconcentratedstock.com, email **info@unwindingconcentratedstock.com**, or connect directly on

LinkedIn.

Made in the USA
Monee, IL
05 November 2026

67814347R00138